Wort für Wort

German vocabulary for AQA A-level

Paul Stocker

HODDER
...TION...
...K COMPANY

Acknowledgements

The author would like to thank Mathias Mendyka, Evelyn Schmitz and Martin Fries for their invaluable help in preparing this book, and for their many useful suggestions. I should also like to thank Ivette Miller for her invaluable help and many helpful suggestions in preparing the latest editions of this book.

Every effort has been made to trace all copyright holders, but if any have been inadvertently overlooked, the Publishers will be pleased to make the necessary arrangements at the first opportunity.

Although every effort has been made to ensure that website addresses are correct at time of going to press, Hodder Education cannot be held responsible for the content of any website mentioned in this book. It is sometimes possible to find a relocated web page by typing in the address of the home page for a website in the URL window of your browser.

Hachette UK's policy is to use papers that are natural, renewable and recyclable products and made from wood grown in sustainable forests. The logging and manufacturing processes are expected to conform to the environmental regulations of the country of origin.

Orders: please contact Bookpoint Ltd, 130 Park Drive, Milton Park, Abingdon, Oxon OX14 4SE. Telephone: (44) 01235 827720. Fax: (44) 01235 400401. E-mail: education@bookpoint.co.uk Lines are open from 9 a.m. to 5 p.m., Monday to Saturday, with a 24-hour message-answering service. You can also order through our website: www.hoddereducation.co.uk

ISBN: 978 1 5104 3484 4

Cover photo © imageBROKER/Alamy Stock Photo
Typeset in India
Printed in CPI Group (UK) Ltd, Croydon, CR0 4YY

A catalogue record for this title is available from the British Library.

MIX
Paper from
responsible sources
FSC™ C104740

Contents

Introduction

This new AQA edition of *Wort für Wort* brings further revisions to reflect recent changes in the AQA AS and A-level examination specifications and contemporary topics.

The core of the book consists of vocabulary lists relating to four major AQA themes, each of which is divided into three sections, each covering a topic from the AQA specification. These are divided further into specific social and cultural topics. At the start of each topic there is a shaded section of revision vocabulary, followed by a list of single vocabulary items in alphabetical order, finishing with longer phrases to provide a context and a 'feel' for the way language is used; you can, of course, extract individual nouns or verbs from this to use in a different context.

At the end of each topic you will find (a) some useful websites, which deal with or provide links to aspects of the particular topic, and (b) two or three exercises based on the relevant topic, which practise the vocabulary listed therein, together with some strategies to help you to learn it.

General sections A–E are either new or updated:
- **Section A Ich meine, ...** lists words and short phrases for use in discussions (under 'A1 Einfache Ausdrücke / Simple expressions'), then longer items for use in written work (under 'A2 Längere Ausdrücke / Longer phrases').
- **Section B Film and literature** contains a range of vocabulary to support essay-writing on film and literature which will be useful for the essay you have to write on your chosen film or piece of literature.
- **Section C Research and presentation** contains three extra lists on the topics of Sport, the Environment and Education, which are not included in the AQA specification; should you choose one of these topics for the Individual Research Project (examined orally), the vocabulary could give you useful support.
- **Section D Welches Wort soll ich wählen?** lists key words for which English speakers often find it difficult to select the most appropriate German equivalent.
- **Section E Zeitausdrücke** provides some useful time phrases.

The topics covered match those in the AQA A-level specification and as such they are ideal to use alongside any textbook for the course, particularly in order to prepare for your oral examination. All theme-based vocabulary has been included with the aim of using it in an oral register.

Alternatively, this book can be used as a study aid to extend the breadth of your vocabulary on each of the topics covered, although it is not a dictionary or an encyclopaedia.

Learning vocabulary

Building one's active vocabulary quickly and efficiently (which also means remembering it!) is a major concern. Here is one technique for doing so. Always learn vocabulary at the beginning of a work session while you are still fresh.

1 Sit in a quiet place. No background music for this work!
2 Read each German–English pair of words or phrases aloud, twice, including gender and plural forms (if it's a noun), concentrating hard on the spelling as you do so.
3 After five pairs, cover up the English side of the page, and repeat the five pairs aloud again.
4 As stage 3, but this time cover the German side. Write the words out.
5 After 20 pairs, repeat stage 4. Repeat stages 3 and 4 after two hours, and again the next day. Give yourself a written test.

With practice, you will be able to learn 20–30 words in 10–15 minutes, and remember almost all of them weeks later.

Developing your vocabulary

Language is constantly changing. Jot down new words and expressions as you hear or read them; try to use the items in conversation or writing while they are still fresh.

Abbreviations in this book

Acc	Accusative
adj. noun	noun which works like an adjective
conj	conjunction
Dat	Dative
etw.	etwas
Gen	Genitive
inf	informal, colloquial
insep	inseparable verb
invar	invariable case ending
irreg	irregular verb
itr	intransitive verb
jdm.	*jemandem*; shows that the verb or preposition takes the dative
jdn.	*jemanden*; shows that the verb or preposition takes the accusative
o.s.	oneself
pej	pejorative
pf	perfect tense
pl	plural
sing	singular
s.o.	someone
sth.	something
tr	transitive verb
*	perfect tense formed with *sein*

The vowel changes of strong verbs are given in brackets after the infinitive, e.g. *geben (i-a-e)*.

Feminine forms of professions etc. are, for simplicity's sake, only included where they vary from the usual addition of -*in* to the masculine form.

Where there are closely related alternative spelling forms, e.g. *die Fake News* and *die Fakenews*, only the version recommended by Duden is listed.

Paul Stocker

Useful websites

One word of warning: when you search on Google, many of the websites that appear are blogs and tend to be less accurate in terms of spelling and grammar. It is, therefore, advisable to refer to websites of recognised newspapers, magazines or governmental sites, which will be more reliable.

Allgemeine Seiten	General websites
www.goethe.de	*The Goethe-Institut; information for all learners of German*
www.tatsachen-ueber-deutschland.de	*Facts about all aspects of Germany*
www.gfds.de	*Gesellschaft für deutsche Sprache; German language*
www.deutschland.de	*Germany portal*
www.bpb.de	*Bundeszentrale für politische Bildung; information on all aspects of German society, not only political*
www.zdf.de	*Zweites Deutsches Fernsehen; daily news (including heute Xpress) and many other programmes*
www.dw.com	*Deutsche Welle; radio and television, with excellent podcasts and many other resources*

Most translation websites and many online dictionaries are very poor, and lack the detail you need to make informed decisions. These dictionaries have been found to be among the best:

Online-Wörterbücher	Online dictionaries
www.linguee.com	*Instantly shows examples of words and phrases from real texts and advises on the most frequently used terms*
www.dict.leo.org	*Also has useful discussion forums for tricky terms*

Answers

Answers to the end-of-topic activities can be found at:
www.hoddereducation.co.uk/A level vocab

Section A

A1 Einfache Ausdrücke

Simple expressions

A1.1 20 Grundausdrücke

20 basic expressions

außerdem	apart from that; moreover
das mag sein, aber ...	that may be true, but...
das stimmt (nicht)	that's (not) true
deswegen	that's why
eigentlich	actually
einerseits / andererseits	on the one / the other hand
erstens	firstly
es geht um ...	it's a question of...
ich bin dafür / dagegen, dass ...	I'm in favour of / against...
ich meine, ...	I think that...
im Großen und Ganzen	on the whole
im Vergleich zu ...	in comparison to...
jeder weiß, dass ...	everyone knows that...
meiner Meinung nach	in my opinion
natürlich	of course
normalerweise	normally
sicher	certainly
Was hältst du von ...?	What do you think of...?
Wie kommst du darauf?	What makes you think that?
zum Beispiel (z. B.)	for example (e.g.)

A1.2 Erstens, zweitens

Firstly, secondly

am Anfang / zu Anfang	initially
das Pro und Kontra	the pros and cons
erstens, zunächst	first/ly
schließlich	finally
später	later
von vorn	from scratch, from the beginning
zum Abschluss	in conclusion
zweitens	secondly

A1.3 Dazu kommt noch ...

What is more,...

auch	also
dazu	in addition
und dazu kommt noch, dass ...	and, what is more,...
nicht nur ..., sondern auch ...	not only..., but also...
übrigens	incidentally, by the way
was ich eigentlich sagen wollte, ist ...	what I actually mean is...
weiterhin	in addition

A1.4 Zum Beispiel

For example

beispielsweise	for example (e.g.)
bekanntlich	it is known that
das heißt (d. h.)	that is (i.e.)
es stimmt, dass ...	it is true that...
folgendermaßen	as follows
in Bezug auf (+Acc)	with reference to
in diesem Zusammenhang	in this context
nämlich	viz., namely
die Tatsachen	the facts
unter anderem (u. a.)	among other things
wie	such as

A1.5 Weil

Because

also, daher	therefore, so
da (*conj*)	since, as
dadurch, deshalb, deswegen	in that way, because of that, that is why
das hatte zur Folge, dass ...	the result of this was...
das liegt daran, dass ...	that's because...
folglich	consequently, as a result
schon die Tatsache, dass ...	the very fact that...
schon weil ...	if only because...
solange (*conj*)	as / so long as
soweit ich weiß	as / so far as I know
Ursache und Wirkung	cause and effect
wegen (+Gen)	because of (sth.)

A1.6 Vor allem

Above all, notably

ausgerechnet, als / wenn ...	just when...
ausgerechnet er	he of all people
ausnahmslos	without exception
äußerst	extremely

Ich meine, ...

bei Weitem (das Beste)	by far and away (the best)
bei Weitem nicht (so gut wie)	nowhere near (as good as)
besonders; zumal	in particular; especially as
betonen	to emphasise
durchaus	absolutely, definitely
eben; halt	just, simply
es steht fest, dass …	what is sure is that…
ganz und gar	completely, utterly
genau das	especially this
hauptsächlich	notably, mainly
in jeder Hinsicht	in every respect
keineswegs	not at all, not in the least
möglichst (bald)	as (soon) as possible
umso mehr, als	all the more, considering / as
umso wichtiger	all the more important
(das musst du) unbedingt (machen)	(you) really (must do that)
unbestritten ist, dass …	it's not disputed that…
völlig, vollkommen	completely
das Wichtigste ist …	the key issue is…

A1.7 Da habe ich Zweifel — *I'm not so sure*

abgesehen davon, dass …	quite apart from the fact that…
allenfalls; bestenfalls	at best
allerdings	even so / mind you
angeblich	supposedly, allegedly
auf den ersten Blick	at first sight
bis zu einem gewissen Grad(e)	to some extent
da habe ich Zweifel	I have my doubts there
einigermaßen	to some extent
es kommt darauf an, was …	it depends on what…
es sei denn, …	unless…
gewissermaßen	in a way
ich habe den Eindruck, dass …	my impression is that…
kaum	hardly
keinesfalls	under no circumstances
lediglich	merely, simply
praktisch; quasi	virtual(-ly)
relativ	relatively
selbst wenn	even if
teilweise	partly

vermutlich	presumably
Zweifel (*pl*) ausdrücken	to express doubts, reservations

A1.8 Im Vergleich
In comparison

ähnlich (+*Dat*)	similar to, like
als je zuvor	than ever before
ebenso	likewise
genauso	just the same
genauso wichtig	just as important
Kannst du das näher erklären?	Can you explain that more fully?
noch wichtiger ist …	even more important is…
noch (bedeutender)	(even) more (significantly)
sogar	even (more)
sowie	as well as
vergleichen (ei-i-i)	to compare
verglichen mit (+*Dat*)	(when) compared with

A1.9 Im Gegenteil
On the contrary

aber / jedoch	however
alternativ / andernfalls	alternatively
auf der einen / anderen Seite	on the one / other hand
außer (+*Dat*)	apart from
da haben Sie schon Recht, aber …	you are right there, but…
dabei	at the same time / into the bargain
dagegen	on the other hand
das hat damit nichts zu tun	that has nothing to do with it
das ist aus der Luft gegriffen	that has nothing to do with the facts
das stimmt auf keinen Fall	that's absolutely untrue
doch	however / though (*and to contradict a negative question or statement*)
egal ob …	it doesn't matter whether…
es ist fraglich, ob …	it's questionable whether…
es ist unvorstellbar, dass …	it's inconceivable that…
es kann sein, dass …	it may be true that…
freilich	admittedly
immerhin	all the same
in der Tat	in fact
in Wirklichkeit	in reality, in actual fact
mag sein, aber … (*inf*)	that may well be, but…

na schön, aber …	that's all very well, but…
obwohl (*conj*)	although
praktisch ⎫ in der Praxis ⎭	in practice
problematisch dabei ist …	the problem with it is…
sonst	otherwise
stattdessen	instead
trotz (+*Gen*)	in spite of
trotzdem; dennoch	nevertheless, despite this
überhaupt	anyway
während (*conj*)	whereas
was … angeht,	as for…,
wer das glaubt, …	anyone who believes that…
zugegeben; zwar	admittedly

A1.10 Meiner Meinung nach   *In my opinion*

daran gibt es keinen Zweifel	there can be no doubt about that
du musst doch einsehen, dass …	you must agree that…
es geht darum, ob …	it is a question of whether…
es geht um (+*Acc*)	it is a question of (sth.)
es ist offensichtlich, dass … ⎫ es versteht sich von selbst, dass … ⎭	it is obvious that…
es steht fest, dass …	it is certain that…
größtenteils	in the main
im Allgemeinen	in general
im Grunde genommen	basically, essentially
in der Regel	as a rule
klar	clearly
kurz gesagt	in brief
kurz und gut	in a nutshell
offensichtlich	evidently
ohne Zweifel	undeniably
selbstverständlich	of course
Was sagst du zum Problem von …?	What's your view on the problem of…?
Welche Einstellung hast du zu …?	What's your attitude to…?
Wie ist deine Meinung?	What's your opinion?
zweifellos	doubtless

A1.11 Schließlich   *Finally*

| Das sage ich auch! | I think so too! |
| die beste Lösung | the best solution |

ehrlich gesagt	to be honest with you
es ist alles andere als ...	it is anything but…
es ist schade, dass …	it is a pity that…
es ist unbegreiflich, dass …	it is inconceivable that…
es scheint, als ob …	it would seem that…
Ganz meine Meinung!	That's just what I think!
Genau!	Exactly!
glücklicherweise	fortunately
ich bin davon überzeugt, dass …	I'm convinced that…
ich schlage vor, (dass …)	I suggest (that…)
leider	unfortunately
mir scheint es so, als ob …	it seems to me that…
offen gestanden	quite frankly
ohnehin	anyway
schlicht und einfach	plainly and simply
Schlüsse ziehen (*irreg*)	to draw conclusions
So ist es!	That's right!
zu einem Kompromiss kommen* (o-a-o)	to reach a compromise
zum Schluss	in conclusion

A1.12 Weitere nützliche Ausdrücke
Other useful phrases

an sich	actually, on the whole
dadurch	in that way, because of that
dafür	in return, in exchange
irgendjemand	someone or other
irgendwann	(at) some time or other
irgendwas	something (or other)
irgendwie	somehow (or other)
irgendwo(hin)	(to) somewhere or other
meistens	mostly, more often than not
mindestens	at least
nach und nach	bit by bit
ohne Weiteres	straight away, without a second thought
sozusagen	so to speak
stellenweise	in places, here and there
teilweise	partly, in part
unerhört	incredible, outrageous
ungewöhnlich	unusual(-ly)
vielleicht	perhaps

Ich meine, ...

wahrscheinlich	probably
was … betrifft	as far as…is concerned
weitgehend	largely

A2 Längere Ausdrücke

Longer phrases

aus diesem Grund	for that reason
das geht uns alle an	it concerns us all
ein umstrittenes Problem	a controversial issue
es fehlt oft an (+*Dat*)	there is often a lack of…
es steht außer Zweifel, dass …	it is beyond doubt that…
ich bin davon überzeugt, dass …	I am convinced that…
im Gegenteil	on the contrary
um ein einzelnes Beispiel zu nennen	to take a single example
wenn man alles in Betracht zieht	all things considered
wenn wir es genauer betrachten	if we look at it more closely
wir dürfen nicht vergessen, dass …	we must not forget that…

A2.1 Einleitung

Introduction

alle sind sich darüber einig, dass …	everyone is agreed that…
an dieser viel diskutierten Frage scheiden sich die Geister	opinions are divided on this vexed question
angenommen, dass …	assuming that…
darüber wird heftig diskutiert	it has provoked a lot of discussion
das Für und Wider ⎫ das Pro und Kontra ⎭	the pros and cons
die Auseinandersetzung über (+*Acc*)	the argument about…
die Meinungen über (+*Acc*) … gehen weit auseinander	opinions about…differ widely
eine heftige öffentliche Diskussion auslösen	to arouse intense public debate
eine heikle Frage	a thorny question
es ist zum Thema geworden	it has become an issue
es wird oft von anderen Themen in den Hintergrund gedrängt	it is often pushed into the background by the other issues
gehen wir davon aus, dass …	let's assume that…
in vielerlei Hinsicht	in many respects
Ist das zu rechtfertigen?	Can this be justified?
Kritiker bemängeln, dass …	critics point out that…

man gewinnt häufig den Eindruck, dass ...	one often gets the impression that...
man könnte meinen, dass ...	one might think that...
plädieren für (+Acc)	to speak up for
wir begeben uns auf gefährliches Terrain	we're entering a minefield
wir müssen uns damit auseinandersetzen, was ...	we must tackle the problem of what...

A2.2 These — *Arguments for*

auf viel Kritik stoßen* (ö-ie-o)	to encounter a great deal of criticism
auf Widerstand stoßen* (ö-ie-o)	to meet with resistance
dank (+Gen or Dat)	thanks to
darauf wollen wir später zurückkommen	we shall return to this later
das Auffallende ist, dass ...	the striking thing is that...
das muss man als wichtiges Anliegen erkennen	this must be recognised as an important area of concern
das Problem hat besorgniserregende Ausmaße erreicht	the problem has reached worrying proportions
die Folgen werden leicht unterschätzt	it is easy to underestimate the consequences
die Lage ...	the situation...
erregt weiterhin Besorgnis	continues to cause concern
wird dadurch erschwert, dass ...	is made worse by...
wird schlechter	is getting worse
die Sache auf die Spitze treiben	to bring matters to a head
es ist leicht zu ersehen, dass ...	it is easy to see that...
es ist nicht zu leugnen, dass ...	one cannot deny that...
es wird zunehmend erkannt, dass ...	it is increasingly recognised that...
etwas stimmt nicht mit (+Dat) ...	there's something wrong with...
vom politischen Standpunkt aus gesehen	from the political point of view
was Sorgen (pl) bereiten sollte, ist ...	what should cause concern is...
wir legen zu viel Wert auf (+Acc) ...	we attach too much importance to...

A2.3 Antithese — *Arguments against*

allerdings sollte man ...	however, we should...
dagegen lässt sich einwenden, dass ...	one objection to this is that...
das ist nur selten der Fall	that is only rarely the case
das ist zum Scheitern verurteilt	it is condemned to failure

Ich meine, ...

das sollte man mit einem gewissen Argwohn betrachten	one should view this with some mistrust
die Gründe sind noch nicht endgültig geklärt	the reasons have not yet been fully explained
die Sache hat einen Haken	there is a snag
dies will nicht heißen, dass ...	this does not mean that…
dieser Auffassung kann ich nicht zustimmen	I cannot accept this view
einer Sache (*Dat*) im Weg stehen (*irreg*)	to be a stumbling block to sth.
er geht von falschen Voraussetzungen aus	he is arguing from false assumptions
es erwies sich als falsch	it turned out to be wrong
es gibt keinen Anlass zu (+*Dat*) / für (+*Acc*) ...	there are no grounds for…
es kann leicht vorkommen, dass ...	it can easily happen that…
ganz abgesehen davon ...	quite apart from that…
geschweige denn ...	not to mention…
man könnte annehmen, dass ...	one might assume that…
seine Argumente kann man nicht für bare Münze nehmen	you can't take his arguments at face value
wir können uns der Tatsache nicht verschließen, dass ...	we cannot ignore the fact that…

A2.4 Gründe angeben / *Giving reasons*

aller Wahrscheinlichkeit nach	by the law of averages / in all probability
aus folgenden Gründen	for the following reasons
aus politischen Gründen	for political reasons
gelten (i-a-o) für	to be true of
das gilt auch für ...	the same is also true of…
das kann man an einem Beispiel verdeutlichen / belegen	an example will illustrate this
die Sache auf die Spitze treiben (ei-ie-ie)	to bring matters to a head
die Statistik macht deutlich, dass ...	the statistics show clearly that…
die Zahl wird auf ... geschätzt	the number is estimated at…
es ist erwiesen, dass ...	it is a proven fact that…
es wird geschätzt, dass ...	it is estimated that…
in dieser / mancher Hinsicht	in this / many respect(s)
laut Bundeskanzler	according to the Federal Chancellor (= Prime Minister)
laut (+*Gen* or *Dat*) Gesetz	according to the law
man muss darauf hinweisen, dass ...	one must point out that…

man vergleiche …	let us compare…
nach Erkenntnissen (+Gen)	according to the findings of…
nach fachmännischen Schätzungen	according to expert estimates
wie oben erwähnt	as mentioned above

A2.5 Schlussfolgerungen ziehen

Drawing conclusions

alles in allem	all things considered
das Entscheidende dabei ist …	the decisive factor in this is…
das ist erst möglich, wenn …	that is only possible if…
das kleinere Übel	the lesser evil
die Aufgabe ist es / besteht darin, …	the task is,…
die richtigen Prioritäten setzen	to get one's priorities right
die Stichhaltigkeit des Arguments	the validity of the argument
diese Einzelmaßnahmen müssen mit (+Dat) … gekoppelt sein	these individual measures must be linked to…
ein Ziel im Auge behalten (ä-ie-a)	to keep an aim in mind
einfache Lösungen gibt es nicht	there are no easy solutions
es bleibt uns nichts anderes übrig, als …	we have no alternative but to…
es lässt sich daraus schließen, dass …	we can conclude from that that…
es verlangt eine Veränderung unserer Einstellungen	it demands a change in our attitudes
ich bin der Ansicht, dass …	I think that…
man kommt unweigerlich zu dem Schluss, dass …	one is forced to the conclusion that…
man sollte sich vor Augen halten, dass …	we should not lose sight of the fact that…
Tatsachen ins Auge sehen (ie-a-e)	to face the facts
um diesen Gefahren vorzubeugen	in order to avert these dangers
um dieses Ziel zu erreichen	to achieve this goal
zum Scheitern verurteilt	condemned to failure

Ich meine, …

Theme 1

Aspects of German-speaking society

1 Familie im Wandel

mit jdm. ausgehen* (*irreg*)	to go out with s.o.
das Baby (-s)	baby
der Bekannte (*adj. noun*)	friend / acquaintance
die Beziehung (-en)	relationship
die Ehe (-n)	marriage
die Ehefrau (-en)	wife
der Ehemann (¨er)	husband
das Ehepaar (-e)	married couple
die Eltern	parents
der Erwachsene (*adj. noun*)	adult
erziehen (*irreg*)	to bring up (child)
der Freund (-e)	(male) friend, boy-friend
die Freundin (-nen)	(female) friend, girl-friend
geschieden	divorced
die Geschwister (*pl*)	brothers and sisters
getrennt	separated
sich (un)glücklich fühlen	to feel (un-)happy
heiraten	to marry
heterosexuell / homosexuell	heterosexual / homosexual
jdn. kennenlernen	to meet, get to know s.o.
das Kind (-er)	child
die Kindheit	childhood
ledig	single, unmarried
die Liebe	love
die Persönlichkeit	character
die Scheidung (-en)	divorce
schwanger	pregnant
sympathisch	nice, easy to get on with
die Traumfrau / der Traummann	ideal partner
verheiratet	married
sich gut verstehen (*irreg*) miteinander gut auskommen* (o-a-o)	to get on well with each other
der Verwandte (*adj. noun*)	relative
zusammenleben	to live together

1.1 Beziehungen innerhalb der Familie

Family relationships

Eltern und Kinder	*Parents and children*
die Adoleszenz	adolescence
der Erziehungsberechtigte (*adj. noun*)	parent, legal guardian
die Großfamilie (-n)	extended family
ein Kind adoptieren	to adopt a child
ein Kind erziehen (*irreg*)	to bring up a child
ein Kind verwöhnen	to spoil a child
Kinder (*pl*) großziehen (*irreg*)	to raise a family
der Kinderfreibetrag	child allowance
die Kinderjahre	years of childhood
das Kindermädchen (-)	nanny
im Kindesalter	at an early age
die Kindesmisshandlung	child abuse
kindgerecht	suitable for children
die Kleinfamilie (-n) ⎱ die Kernfamilie (-n) ⎰	small (nuclear) family
die Pflegeeltern	foster parents
das Pflegekind (-er)	foster child
der Schwager (⁻)	brother-in-law
die Schwägerin (-nen)	sister-in-law
die Schwiegereltern	parents-in-law
die Stiefmutter (⁻) / der Stiefvater (⁻)	stepmother / stepfather
streng	strict
die Tagesmutter (⁻)	childminder
taufen	to christen
die Zwillinge (*pl*)	twins

sie ist ein gut erzogenes Kind	she's a well-brought-up child
die Verantwortung für Entscheidungen teilen	to share responsibility for decisions
die Verwandtschaft	family (all relatives)
von Kind auf	from childhood
seine Beziehung zu seinem Vater	his relationship with his father
immer mehr Ehen bleiben kinderlos	more and more marriages remain childless
die Schaffung emotionaler Geborgenheit	the creation of a sense of emotional security
die leiblichen Eltern	biological parents
die Eltern müssen lernen, loszulassen	parents have to learn to let go

Teenager über Eltern	*Teenagers talking about parents*
halten (ä-ie-a) für …	to consider (s.o.) to be…
sie hält ihre Eltern für …	she considers her parents to be…
altmodisch	old-fashioned
autoritär	authoritarian
engstirnig	narrow-minded
gerecht	fair
gestresst	stressed
heuchlerisch	hypocritical
(in)tolerant	(in)tolerant
kleinlich	petty
kompromissbereit	ready to compromise
naiv	naïve
peinlich	embarrassing
scheinheilig	hypocritical
streng	strict
verkalkt (*inf*), muffelig (*inf*)	senile, fuddy-duddy, grumpy
verständnislos	unsympathetic
voreingenommen (gegen)	prejudiced (against)
wohlmeinend	well-meaning
nerven	to annoy
schimpfen	to get cross
strafen	to punish
das Verständnis	understanding
sich vertragen (ä-u-a) mit (+*Dat*)	to get on well with
vorwurfsvoll	reproachful

er geht mir auf die Nerven	he gets on my nerves
ich kann mit ihnen über alles reden	I can talk to them about anything
ich komme nur schwer mit (+*Dat*) … zurecht	I find it hard to cope with…
kleinliche Vorschriften	petty rules
man muss Respekt vor Älteren haben	you must respect your elders
meine Eltern bestehen darauf, dass …	my parents insist that…
Respekt zeigen vor (+*Dat*)	to respect
sie hat geschimpft, weil ich …	she told me off, because I…
sie können sich in meine Lage versetzen	they can put themselves in my shoes
sie nörgeln immer an mir herum	they're always nagging me
sie sind stolz auf mich	they're proud of me
sie verstehen sich gut	they get on well together

Eltern über Teenager

Eltern über Teenager	*Parents talking about teenagers*
sich schlecht benehmen (*irreg*)	to behave badly
jdn. beschimpfen	to swear at s.o.
die Clique	one's group of friends
die Emotionen, Empfindungen	feelings, emotions
fluchen	to use bad language, to swear
gebildet	well-bred, educated
kultiviert, fein	sophisticated, refined
lächerlich	ludicrous, ridiculous
meine Eltern halten mich für …	my parents think I'm…
apathisch	apathetic
ausweichend	evasive
deprimiert	depressed
ehrgeizig	ambitious
gesellig	sociable, gregarious
gleichgültig	indifferent
gut angepasst	well-adjusted
hartnäckig	stubborn
hilfsbereit	helpful
launisch	moody
planlos	lacking in direction
überempfindlich	oversensitive
ungezogen	ill-mannered
(un)höflich	(im)polite
unsicher, verunsichert	insecure, uncertain
verantwortungsbewusst	responsible
niedergeschlagen sein* (*irreg*)	to feel low
verlegen	embarrassed

ich bin immer der / die Böse	I'm always the bad guy
du nimmst deine Arbeit auf die leichte Schulter	you're not taking your work seriously enough
du willst das eine haben und das andere nicht lassen	you want it both ways
er kommt mit seinem Vater schlecht zurecht	he doesn't get on with his father
gute Manieren haben (*irreg*)	to have good manners
in den frühen Morgenstunden nach Hause kommen* (o-a-o)	to come home in the small hours
in den Tag hinein leben	to live for the day
sich in seiner Haut wohlfühlen	to feel good about o.s.

sie ist in der Pubertät	she's at that awkward adolescent stage
sich über etw. / jdn. lustig machen	to make fun of sth. / s.o.
sie malt alles schwarzweiß	she sees everything in black and white
auf Äußerlichkeiten fixiert	obsessed with appearances
sich sonderbar kleiden	to dress outlandishly
die Verantwortung tragen (ä-u-a)	to take responsibility
alles in Frage stellen	to question everything
auf die schiefe Bahn geraten* (ä-ie-a)	to go off the rails
aus dem eigenen Schaden lernen	to learn the hard way
das ist einzig und allein meine Sache	that's a matter for me alone
die Autorität in Frage stellen	to challenge authority

Der Konflikt	*Conflict*
angespannt	tense
ärgern	to annoy
ausziehen* (*irreg*)	to move out
beleidigen	to insult
enttäuscht	disappointed
meckern	to moan, grumble
minderjährig	under-age
nachtragend sein* (*irreg*)	to bear grudges
reagieren auf (+*Acc*)	to react (to)
jdn. reizen	to provoke s.o.
streiten (ei-i-i)	to argue, squabble
die Streitigkeiten	arguments
taktlos	tactless
ungelöst	unresolved
sich wieder vertragen (ä-u-a)	to make it up (get along again)
jdm. (etw.) verzeihen (ei-ie-ie)	to forgive s.o. (for sth.)
zugeben (i-a-e)	to concede

die Beherrschung verlieren (ie-o-o)	to lose one's temper
bei etw. (+*Dat*) ein Auge zudrücken	to turn a blind eye to sth.
wir besprechen Probleme gemeinsam	we talk problems over together
Ich bin nicht von gestern!	I wasn't born yesterday!
auf jdn. böse werden* (i-u-o) / sein* (*irreg*)	to get / be angry with s.o.
über etw. böse werden* (i-u-o) / sein* (*irreg*)	to get / be angry at sth.
ich falle mit der Tür ins Haus	I'll come straight to the point

sie gehen in die Luft (*inf*)	they fly off the handle, lose their rag
sie geht mir auf die Nerven	she gets on my nerves
es gibt Krach wegen …	there's trouble about…
viel Lärm um nichts	a storm in a teacup
das lasse ich mir nicht mehr gefallen	I won't put up with it any more
lass uns offen reden	let's be open about this
sie lässt sich von ihren Eltern nichts sagen	she won't be told anything by her parents
wir reden in aller Ruhe darüber	we talk about it quietly
Das mache ich nicht mit!	I just won't stand for it!
ein Problem in einem offenen Gespräch lösen	to deal with a problem openly
Rechte und Pflichten	rights and responsibilities
sie reden nicht mehr miteinander	they're not talking to one another
mir reißt die Geduld / der Geduldsfaden	my patience is wearing thin
sie haben sich gestritten	they've had a quarrel, an argument
wir stimmen nicht überein	we don't agree
seinen Willen durchsetzen	to get one's own way
viel Wind um etw. machen	to make a fuss about sth.
ein wunder Punkt	a sore point
wütend reagieren	to react angrily
ich ziehe die Grenze bei (+*Dat*)	I draw the line at…

Charakter – Positives — *Character – positive points*

der Altruismus	altruism
anpassungsfähig	adaptable
anständig	respectable
aufgeschlossen	open-minded
begeistert	enthusiastic
bescheiden / die Bescheidenheit	modest / modesty
ehrgeizig / der Ehrgeiz	ambitious / ambition
ehrlich / die Ehrlichkeit	honest / honesty
die Eigenschaft (-en)	characteristic
extravagant	flamboyant
extrovertiert	extrovert
fleißig	hard-working
geduldig / die Geduld	patient / patience
gehorsam / der Gehorsam	obedient / obedience
großzügig / die Großzügigkeit	generous / generosity
idealistisch / der Idealismus	idealistic / idealism

kinderlieb	fond of children
kontaktfreudig	outgoing
lebhaft, temperamentvoll	lively, vivacious
lieb / liebevoll	kind
liebenswürdig / die Liebenswürdigkeit	kind / kindness
offen / die Offenheit	open / openness
rücksichtsvoll	considerate
ruhig	calm
selbstbewusst	confident
selbstständig / die Selbstständigkeit	independent / independence
sensibel	sensitive
sparsam / die Sparsamkeit	thrifty / thriftiness
treu / die Treue	faithful/ness, loyal/ty
unternehmungslustig	enterprising, adventurous
vernünftig / die Vernunft	sensible / common sense
verständnisvoll	understanding
zielstrebig	determined, focused
das Zuhören-Können	the ability to listen
zurückhaltend	reserved
zuverlässig / die Zuverlässigkeit	reliable / reliability

einen guten Eindruck machen	to make a good impression
er ist lebensfroh	he enjoys life
er hat Humor	he's got a good sense of humour
gute Manieren haben (*irreg*)	to be well-behaved
jeder Mensch hat etwas ganz Besonderes	everyone has something special about them

Charakter – Negatives	*Character – negative points*
aggressiv	aggressive
angespannt	tense
anstrengend	demanding
arrogant / die Arroganz	arrogant, arrogance
sich beschweren	to complain
besorgt	anxious
blöd	stupid, idiotic
boshaft	malicious
brummig, mürrisch	cantankerous, grumpy
denkfaul	mentally lazy
deprimiert / die Depression	depressed / depression

der Egoismus	selfishness
egoistisch, selbstsüchtig	selfish
er nimmt sich selbst zu ernst	he takes himself too seriously
faul	lazy
sich für jdn. fremdschämen	to find s.o. cringeworthy, to cringe for s.o.
geizig	mean (miserly)
gemein	mean (unkind)
die Hemmungen	inhibitions
im Stress sein* (irreg)	to be under stress
das Labermaul ⎤ die Klatschtante ⎦	chatterbox, blabbermouth
lügen (ü-o-o)	to lie, tell lies
nervig	annoying
reizbar	irritable
schmuddelig	sloppy
schüchtern	shy
unbeherrscht	lacking self-control
unehrlich / die Unehrlichkeit	dishonest / dishonesty
ungehorsam / der Ungehorsam	disobedient / disobedience
unsozial	antisocial
unverschämt	outrageous, impudent
verantwortungslos	irresponsible
verklemmt	inhibited
verschlossen	withdrawn
vulgär	vulgar
wahnsinnig	mad, crazy

1.2 Partnerschaft und Ehe   *Partnership and marriage*

Die Freundschaft	*Friendship*
akzeptiert werden* (i-u-o)	to be accepted
sich anpassen (+Dat)	to fit in with, conform to
ausgrenzen	to exclude
die Clique (-n)	group of friends
der Gruppenzwang	peer pressure
gleichaltrig	of the same age
sich mit jdm. herumtreiben (ei-ie-ie)	to hang out with s.o. (friends)
der Jugendliche (adj. noun)	adolescent, young person
mobben	to bully

Spaß haben (*irreg*)	to have fun
sich auf seine Freunde verlassen (ä-ie-a)	to rely on one's friends
das Vertrauen	trust

Die Liebe — *Love*

jdn. ansprechen (i-a-o) } jdn. anquatschen (*inf*) }	to chat s.o. up
anziehend } reizend }	attractive
jdn. aufreißen (ei-i-i) (*inf*)	to 'pull' s.o. (*inf*)
die Beziehung (-en)	relationship
mit jdm. gehen* (*irreg*)	to go out with s.o.
der Geliebte (*adj. noun*)	lover
die große Liebe	the love of one's life, the real thing
gut aussehend	good-looking
mit jdm. schlafen (ä-ie-a)	to sleep, have sex with s.o.
sich in jdn. verlieben	to fall in love with s.o.

---

an seinen Partner hohe Ansprüche stellen	to demand high standards of one's partner
jdn. auf einer Party kennenlernen	to meet s.o. at a party
jdn. durch Online-Dating kennenlernen	to meet s.o. through online dating
jdn. um den Finger wickeln	to wrap s.o. round one's little finger
mit jdm. Schluss machen	to finish with s.o.
Liebe auf den ersten Blick	love at first sight
sich Hals über Kopf in jdn. verlieben	to fall head over heels in love with s.o.
jdm. einen Korb geben (i-a-e)	to finish with s.o.
sie hat Angst davor, sich festzulegen	she's frightened of commitment
das gegenseitige Verständnis	mutual understanding
man sollte über alles sprechen können	you should be able to talk about everything
sie haben vieles gemeinsam	they have a lot in common
verliebt, verlobt, verheiratet	in love, engaged, married (the old norm for families)

Die Ehe — *Marriage*

die Braut (̈-e)	bride
der Bräutigam (-e)	groom
der Ehering (-e)	wedding ring
die Gemeinsamkeit	common ground, togetherness

die Hochzeit (-en)	wedding
der Hochzeitsempfang	wedding reception
die Hochzeitsreise (-n)	honeymoon
der Polterabend	pre-wedding party
sich verloben mit (+*Dat*)	to get engaged to
die Verlobung	engagement
das Vertrauen	trust
die Zärtlichkeit	tenderness
zusammenhalten (ä-ie-a)	to stick together

die kirchliche Trauung	church wedding
sich kirchlich trauen lassen (ä-ie-a)	to get married in church
die standesamtliche Trauung	civil (i.e. legal) ceremony
eine glückliche Ehe führen	to have a happy marriage
bis dass der Tod uns scheidet	till death do us part

Trennung / Scheidung — *Separation / divorce*

der Alleinerziehende (*adj. noun*)	single parent
sich auseinanderleben	to grow apart
ausziehen* (*irreg*)	to move out
jdn. betrügen (ü-o-o)	to cheat on s.o.
die Eheberatung	marriage guidance (counselling)
Ehebruch begehen (*irreg*)	to commit adultery
auf jdn. eifersüchtig sein* (*irreg*)	to feel jealous of s.o.
der Elternteil	(one) parent
fremdgehen* (*irreg*)	to have affairs
sich scheiden lassen (ä-ie-a)	to get divorced
sie haben sich scheiden lassen	they got divorced
die Scheidung (-en)	divorce
der Scheidungsprozess	divorce proceedings
die Scheidungsrate	divorce rate
scheitern*	to break down
der Seitensprung (¨e)	affair outside marriage
das Sorgerecht	custody
sich das Sorgerecht teilen	to share custody (of children)
der Streit (-e)	argument, quarrel
(sich) streiten (ei-i-i)	to argue, quarrel
die Streitigkeiten	quarrels, squabbles
sich trennen, getrennt	to split up, separated

die meisten Geschiedenen (*adj. noun*) heiraten erneut	most divorced people remarry
er will sich nicht gebunden fühlen	he doesn't want any ties
aufgrund der Unvereinbarkeit der Charaktere	on grounds of incompatibility
häufig den Partner wechseln	to sleep around
ihre Ehe ging in die Brüche	their marriage broke up
sie hat ein Kind aus erster Ehe	she has a child from her first marriage
sie leben getrennt	they live apart
sie passen nicht zusammen / zueinander	they're incompatible
sich um die Kinder kümmern	to look after the children
dem Vater wurde das Sorgerecht für das Kind zugesprochen	the father was awarded custody of the child
sie leben finanziell prekär	their lives are financially difficult

Die Schwangerschaft　　　　　　　*Pregnancy*

die Abtreibung (-en) ⎫ der Schwangerschaftsabbruch (ˣe) ⎭	abortion
die Antibabypille (-n)	contraceptive pill
ein Baby stillen	to breast-feed a baby
empfangen (ä-i-a)	to conceive
die Empfängnisverhütung	contraception
der Elternurlaub ⎫ die Elternzeit ⎭	parental leave (on birth of child)
die Familienplanung	family planning
der Fötus (*pl* Föten / Fötusse)	fœtus
die Fristenregelung	law allowing abortion within first 3 months
gebären (ie-a-o)	to give birth to
geboren werden* (i-u-o)	to be born
die Geburt (-en)	birth
die Geburtenkontrolle	birth control
kinderlos	childless
das Kondom (-e)	condom
die Leihmutter (ˣ)	surrogate mother
mütterlich	motherly, maternal
der Mutterschaftsurlaub	maternity leave
der Schwangerschaftstest (-s)	pregnancy test
eine (un)erwünschte Schwangerschaft	a(n) (un)wanted pregnancy

....

ein Kind erwarten	to be expecting a baby
sie bekommt ein Kind	she's having a baby

ein Baby abtreiben lassen (ä-ie-a)	to have an abortion
in gebärfähigem Alter	of child-bearing age
die künstliche Befruchtung	artificial insemination
Mutter werden* (i-u-o)	to have a baby
zur Welt kommen* (o-a-o)	to be born
aus gutem Elternhaus stammen	to come from a good home
der Schutz des ungeborenen Lebens	the protection of the unborn child

1.3 Verschiedene Familienformen

Different types of family

Neue Familienformen	***New forms of family***
alleinerziehend	single (as parent)
alleinstehend	single, unattached
die Aufgaben aufteilen	to share the tasks
der Brotverdiener	bread-winner, main earner
die Bumerangkinder	'boomerang' children
die Einelternfamilie (-n)	single-parent family
die Einkindfamilie (-n)	single-child family
finanziell unabhängig	financially independent
die Gleichberechtigung	equality
ein gleichgeschlechtliches Paar (-e)	same-sex couple
der Halbbruder (¨), die Halbschwester (-n)	half-brother, half-sister
die Homo-Ehe (-n) (*inf*)	same-sex marriage
der Homosexuelle, Schwule (both *adj. noun*) / schwul	homosexual / gay
seine Karriere aufgeben (i-a-e)	to give up one's career
die Kinder betreuen	to look after the children
der Lebensgefährte (-n) / die Lebensgefährtin (-nen)	partner
die Lesbe (-n), die Lesbierin / lesbisch	lesbian
der Neubeginn	fresh start
die nichteheliche Beziehung (-en)	non-marital relationship, cohabitation
die (eingetragene) Partnerschaft (-en)	civil partnership
die Patchworkfamilie (-n)	patchwork family (from divorced families)
die Regenbogenfamilie (-n)	'rainbow' family (same-sex parents)
die Stiefmutter (¨), die Stiefschwester (-n)	step mother, step sister
der Stiefvater (¨), der Stiefbruder (¨)	step-father, step-brother

die traditionelle Familie (-n)	traditional family
der / die Transgender	transgender person
zur Waise werden* (i-u-o)	to be orphaned
die wilde Ehe	co-habitation, living together
das Ziehkind (-er)	foster-child
mit jdm. zusammenziehen* (*irreg*)	to move in with s.o.
zuständig für	responsible for

die Ehe ist auf dem Rückzug	(the institution of) marriage is in retreat
man braucht keinen Trauschein	you don't need a marriage certificate
eine Vielfalt an Lebensformen	a variety of life-styles
der Wandel in unserer Gesellschaft	the change in our society
der Wandel in den Geschlechterrollen	changes in the roles of the sexes
die Familie hat sich gewandelt	the family has changed
Ehen halten immer kürzer	marriages last less and less time
… ist zunehmend akzeptiert	…is increasingly accepted
Homosexuelle (*adj. noun*) werden nicht mehr diskriminiert	homosexuals are no longer discriminated against
zu seinen Eltern zurückziehen* (*irreg*)	to move back in with one's parents

Alt werden

	Getting old
das Altenheim (-e)	old people's home
die Altenpflege	the care of old people
die Altersbeschwerden	infirmities of old age
die Altersversorgung	old-age pension
der Alzheimer	Alzheimer's (disease)
die Autonomie gewährleisten	to guarantee freedom / autonomy
die Behinderung (-en)	disability
das betreute Wohnen	sheltered housing
die Betreuung	looking after (patient / dependent)
an Demenz leiden (*irreg*)	to suffer from dementia
Hotel Mama	family home (too comfortable to leave)
die Lebenserwartung	life expectancy
leiden (*irreg*) an (+*Dat*)	to suffer from
Mehrgenerationenhäuser	family homes made up of several generations
der Nesthocker (-)	person who remains at home for a long time
pflegebedürftig werden* (i-u-o)	to start to need looking after
das Pflegeheim (-e)	care home
die Rente	pension

in (die) Rente gehen* (*irreg*)	to start drawing one's pension
der Rentner (-)	pensioner
die Rund-um-die-Uhr-Betreuung	round-the-clock care
die Selbstständigkeit aufgeben (i-a-e)	to give up one's independence
die Senioren	senior citizens
der Seniorenausweis (-e)	pensioner's bus / rail pass
die Witwe (-n) / der Witwer (-)	widow / widower

das Gefühl, gebraucht zu werden	the feeling that one's needed
das Bedürfnis nach Gemeinschaft	the need for community
in den (Vor)ruhestand treten* (i-a-e)	to take (early) retirement
in hohem Alter fit bleiben* (ei-ie-ie)	to remain fit in old age
in der letzten Lebensphase	in the last stages of one's life
sich an den Ruhestand gewöhnen	to get used to being retired
generationenübergreifendes Wohnen	several generations sharing the same house
Oma passt auf die Enkelkinder auf	Grandma looks after the grandchildren
Frauen werden älter als Männer	women live longer than men
man ist auf Hilfe angewiesen	you're reliant on help
um jdn. trauern	to be in mourning for s.o.
die Radieschen von unten ansehen (ie-a-e)	to be pushing up the daisies

---

Websites

You will find other useful articles, links and vocabulary on this topic on the following websites:

www.bmfsfj.de *Federal Ministry for Families, Senior Citizens, Women and Children*

www.familienhandbuch.de

ACTIVITIES

Strategy
Forming nouns from verbs and adjectives

Nouns are often derived from verbs and adjectives.
● nouns derived from verbs often end with -ung (like English -ing)
● nouns derived from adjectives often end with -heit or -keit (like English -ness)

Both groups of nouns are always feminine.

A Notieren Sie die englische Bedeutung dieser Wörter aus der Vokabelliste. Finden Sie das Basisverb oder -adjektiv für jedes Substantiv.
   1 die Beziehung
   2 die Schönheit
   3 die Scheidung
   4 die Gleichgültigkeit
   5 die Schaffung
   6 die Verantwortung
   7 die Unhöflichkeit
   8 die Beherrschung
   9 die Verlegenheit
   10 die Begeisterung

Strategy
Looking for the roots of complex words

Root words are the base words from which complex words (i.e. with more than one element) may be formed. These 'complex' words always have the root word at the heart of their meaning. When you come across a word which is new to you, look for its root, then at what has been added; this will give a good indication of what the word relates to and, in context, what it means.

B Finden Sie mit Hilfe eines Wörterbuchs die englische Bedeutung dieser Wörter; alle basieren auf dem Wort ‚Liebe'.
   1 lieben
   2 sich verlieben in
   3 beliebt
   4 liebevoll
   5 lieblich
   6 der/die Geliebte
   7 der Liebling
   8 lieb haben
   9 die Hassliebe
   10 die Vorliebe

2 Die digitale Welt

Note that German borrows many words used in the world of computers and the internet directly from English/American, e.g. *chatten, tweeten*. Outside this context, other words are used: *plaudern* (to chat), *zwitschern* (to tweet (birds)).

aktuell	up to date
jdn. anrufen ⎫ mit jdm. telefonieren ⎭	to phone s.o
anschließen (ie-o-o)	to plug in
der Bildschirm (-e)	screen
der Computer (-)	computer
die Daten (*pl*)	data
downloaden ⎫ herunterladen (ä-u-a) ⎭	to download
drucken, der Drucker (-)	to print, printer
einloggen / ausloggen	to log on / log off
einschalten / ausschalten	to switch on / switch off
(ein)tippen	to type (in)
fernsehen (ie-a-e)	to watch TV
funktionieren (*itr*)	to work (machine)
die Gefahr (-en)	danger
gesellig	sociable
im Internet / im Netz	on the internet
der Internetzugang	access to the internet
der / das Laptop (-s)	laptop (computer)
löschen	to delete
jdm. mailen	to e-mail s.o.
die Nachricht / Nachrichten (*pl*)	piece of news / the news
die Neuigkeit (-en)	(latest) news
ein sicheres Passwort	a secure password
die Playlist (-s)	play list
das Smartphone (-s)	smartphone
die SMS (-), jdm. simsen	text message, to text s.o.
die Spielkonsole (-n)	games console
die Startseite (-n)	home page
das Tablet (-s)	tablet (computer)
die Tastatur (-en)	keyboard
uploaden ⎫ hochladen (ä-u-a) ⎭	to upload
die Webseite (n)	web page

2.1 Das Internet   *The internet*

der Abonnent (-en)	subscriber
einen Newsfeed abonnieren	to subscribe to a newsfeed
aktivieren	to activate, enable (a system or feature)
aktualisieren	to update
der Algorithmus (*pl* -rithmen)	algorithm
der Anhang (ꞏ-e)	attachment (e.g. file)
der Anschluss (ꞏ-e)	connection
archivieren	to store
die Audiodatei (-en)	audio file
der / das Computervirus (*pl* -viren)	computer virus
das Darknet	the dark web
die Datei (-en)	file
die Datenbank (-en)	database
der Datenschutz	data protection
der drahtlose Internetzugang	wireless internet access
durchstöbern (*insep*)	to browse
die elektronischen Medien	the electronic media
seine E-Mails lesen (ie-a-e)	to look at one's e-mails
sich erkundigen nach (+*Dat*)	to find out about
ein FaceTime-Gespräch führen	to have a FaceTime conversation
die Geschwindigkeit (-en)	speed
der Gestalter (-)	designer
hacken in (+*Acc*)	to hack into
der / das illegale Download (-s)	illegal download
die Internetanbindung (-en)	internet connection
der Internetbetrug	internet scam
der Internetkonzern (-e)	online company
der Internet-Nutzer (-)	internet user
der Kinderschutz	child protection
die Klickzahl	the number of hits/clicks
der Kommentar (-e)	comment
kostenlos	free
das Lesezeichen (-)	bookmark (in a browser)
der Livestream	live streaming
manipulieren	to manipulate
die Mediathek	media library
etw. nachschlagen	to look sth. up
das Nachrichtenwesen	news media
navigieren	to navigate

der Nutzer (-), Benutzer (-)	user
online einkaufen	to shop online
online sein* (*irreg*)	to be online
das Onlinebanking	online banking
die Onlinedienste	online services
die Pinnwand (¨e)	noticeboard
die Plattform (-en)	platform
die Privatsphäre-Einstellungen	privacy settings
die Raubkopie (-n)	pirated copy
der Reichtum	fortune (money)
der Ruhm	fame
schützen vor (*+Dat*)	to protect from
mit jdm. skypen	to skype s.o.
(zu)spammen	to spam
die Suchmaschine (-n)	search engine
im Internet surfen	to surf the net
auf Tastendruck	at the push of a button
die Unterhaltung	entertainment
vernetzen	to network
veröffentlichen	to publish, make public
die Verschlüsselung	encryption
der Videoanruf (-e) ⎱ das Videotelefonat (-e) ⎰	video call
die Videokonferenz (-en)	video conference
Viren (*pl*) auffinden (i-a-u)	to detect viruses
der Virenscanner (-)	virus scanner
eine Webseite besuchen	to visit a webpage
der / das Werbelink (-s)	advertising link
sein Wissen erweitern	to expand one's knowledge
die Zustimmung	consent
die Zuverlässigkeit	reliability, truthfulness

· ·

ein Video ins Internet stellen	to put a video online
mit Werbung bombardieren	to bombard with advertising
die Informationsgesellschaft	information technology-based society
auf dem Laufenden bleiben* (ei-ie-ie)	to keep up to date
sich durch Werbeeinnahmen (*pl*) finanzieren	to be financed by advertising revenue
durch Webseiten scrollen	to scroll through web pages
er kann mit Computern nichts anfangen	he hasn't a clue about computers

man kann Geräte per Handy einstellen	you can operate devices using your mobile phone

Probleme — *Problems*

der Datendiebstahl	data theft
die Einsamkeit	loneliness
die Entschlüsselung	decryption
die Fake News	fake news
die Gewalt	violence
die Gewaltdarstellung (-en)	depiction of violence
gewaltsam	violent
passiv	passive
peinlich	embarrassing
die Pornografie	pornography
postfaktisch (*adj*)	post-truth
die Scheinwelt	a bogus world
die Sicherheitsmaßnahme (-n)	security measure
der Terrorismus	terrorism
trivial	trivial
die unkritische Haltung	uncritical attitude
vegetieren / vertrotteln (*inf*)	to vegetate
verbreiten	to disseminate
es lässt dich verdummen	it dulls your mind
das Verhalten	behaviour
verharmlosen	to make sth. appear harmless
der Verlust von Fantasie / Fantasieverlust	loss of one's imagination
wertlos	worthless
ohne Zustimmung hochladen (ä-u-a)	to upload without consent

persönliche Daten (*pl*) preisgeben (i-a-e)	to reveal personal information
Besteht ein direkter Zusammenhang zwischen Gewaltdarstellungen (*pl*) und Jugendkriminalität?	Is there a direct link between the depiction of violence and teenage crime?
es steht im Mittelpunkt pädagogischer Kritik	it is at the centre of criticism from educationalists
sie verbringen zu viel Zeit mit Computern (*pl*)	they spend too much time on the computer
Eltern sollten verhindern, dass ihre Kinder …	parents should prevent their children from…

sie beschäftigen sich zu wenig mit ihren Kindern	they take too little interest in their children
anstößige Inhalte (pl) aussortieren	to filter out offensive material
die negative Auswirkung der digitalen Medien auf unser Gehirn	the negative effects of digital media on our brains

Vorteile des Internets	***Advantages of the internet***
die Aktualitat	relevance, topicality
die Anonymität	anonymity
benutzerfreundlich	user-friendly
effizient	efficient
die Geschwindigkeit (-en)	speed
der Informationszugang	access to information
kommunizieren	to communicate
die Kostenersparnisse	cost savings
vereinfachen	to simplify
die Verfügbarkeit	availability
in kürzester Zeit	in next to no time

....

Alles, was Sie brauchen, steht Ihnen zur Verfügung	everything you need is at your fingertips
man spart Zeit und Geld	you save time and money
es ist 24 Stunden erreichbar	it's available 24 hours a day
die globale Kommunikation	global communication
Informationen (pl) austauschen	to exchange information
der pädagogische Nutzen	educational benefits
eine globale Kultur des Teilens und Zusammenarbeitens	a global culture of sharing and co-operation
Vernetzungsmöglichkeiten eröffnen	to open up networking possibilities

2.2 Soziale Netzwerke　　*Social networks*

die Altersbeschränkung	age restriction
die Einsamkeit	loneliness
das Emoji (-s)	emoji
jdn. entfreunden	to unfriend s.o. (on Facebook)
erreichbar	contactable
auf Facebook gehen* (*irreg*) facebooken	to go on Facebook
der Follower (-)	follower (on e.g. Twitter)

die Gefahr (-en)	danger
gefährlich	dangerous
gesponsert	sponsored
das Hashtag (-s)	hashtag
kommunizieren mit (+*Dat*)	to communicate with
mit jdm. in Kontakt treten* (i-a-e) sich mit jdm. in Verbindung setzen	to make contact with s.o.
kontaktfreudig sein* (*irreg*)	to enjoy making contact
leicht zu erreichen	easily accessible / contactable
liken	to 'like'
mailen	to mail
mit jdm. online chatten	to chat with s.o. online
posten	to post
das Profil (-e)	profile
schützen	to protect
taggen	to tag
der Troll (-e)	troll
twittern, (re)tweeten	to (re-)tweet

- -

Kontakte (*pl*) knüpfen	to network
ein Teil des heutigen Lebens	part of everyday life
heute geht es nicht mehr ohne	these days people can't do without it
man ist immer und überall erreichbar	people can always contact you, wherever you are
jdm. etw. ausrichten lassen (ä-ie-a)	to leave s.o. a message

Probleme	***Problems***
die Aufmerksamkeitsspanne	attention span
die Auswirkung (-en) auf (+*Acc*)	the effect on
beeinflussen	to influence
die Brutalität	brutality
der / die Couch-Potato (-s) der Dauerglotzer (-)	couch potato
das Cybermobbing	cyber bullying
die Depression	depression
deprimiert	depressed
der Gruppenzwang	peer pressure
jdn. hänseln	to pick on s.o.
mobben	to bully
der Pädophile (*adj. noun*)	paedophile

die Schikane (-n)	bullying, harassment
die Vereinsamung	loneliness, isolation
Essstörungen verherrlichen	to glorify eating disorders
verleumden	to write malicious things

Kinder kommen übermüdet in die Schule	children are overtired when they arrive in school
sie klebt am Handy	she's glued to her mobile phone
er kontrolliert alle paar Minuten seine Facebook-Seite	he checks his Facebook page every few minutes
Kinder fühlen sich leicht ausgegrenzt	children can easily feel excluded
es beeinflusst unsere Wertvorstellungen	it influences our moral values
negative Kommentare posten	to post negative comments
man sollte keine Kontaktanfragen von Fremden annehmen	you shouldn't accept contact requests from strangers

Vorteile	*Benefits*
Fotos mit Freunden teilen	to share photos with friends
Leute mit ähnlichen Interessen	people with similar interests
man kann kontrollieren, was Freunde posten	you can check what friends have been posting
man kann sich leicht mit anderen verknüpfen	it's easy to link up with other people
mit Freunden in Verbindung bleiben* (ei-ie-ie)	to stay in touch with friends
die Möglichkeit, berufliche Kontakte zu knüpfen	the opportunity to make professional contacts
eine Nachricht sofort senden / bekommen	to send / receive a message instantly
neue Leute kennenlernen	to get to know new people

2.3 Die Digitalisierung der Gesellschaft

The digitalisation of society

der Akku (-s)	battery
die Akkulaufzeit	battery life
die App (-s)	app
archivieren	to store
aufrüsten / upgraden	to upgrade

die Computerkenntnisse (*pl*)	computer literacy
einrichten	to set up
der Energieverbrauch	power consumption
die Entwicklung (-en)	development
die Fernbedienung (-en)	remote control (for television etc.)
die Festplatte (-n)	hard drive
die Forschung	research
das Glasfaserkabel (-)	optical fibre cable
handlich	pocket-sized
die Heimvernetzung	connected home
installieren	to install
integriert	integrated
kinderleicht	child's play
die künstliche Intelligenz (KI)	artificial intelligence (AI)
das Ladegerät (-e)	(battery) charger
das Lesegerät (-e)	e-book reader
das Navi	sat nav
netzwerkfähig	network enabled
der Router (-)	router
eine Schaltfläche anklicken	to click on a button
die Speicherkarte (-n)	memory card
der Speicherplatz	memory capacity
die Steckdose (-n)	plug socket
der Stecker (-)	plug
der Technikfeind (-e)	technophobe
verbinden (i-a-u)	to link, connect
die Werbung	advertising
der Zweck (-e)	purpose

....

fast alle Haushalte verfügen über (+*Acc*) …	almost all homes have…
etw. per Sprachbefehl steuern	to operate by voice command
neue Dienste anbieten	to offer new services
die Welt ändert sich permanent	the world is constantly changing

Das Handy — *The mobile phone*

die Bildschirmauflösung	screen resolution
die Einstellungen	settings
der Empfang	reception
entsperren	to unlock
Fotos aufnehmen (*irreg*)	to take photos

die Freisprechanlage (-n)	hands free kit (for mobile)
die Gebühr (-en)	charge
Geräte drahtlos steuern	to control devices hands-free
handlich	handy
die Handynutzung	mobile phone usage
handysüchtig	addicted to one's mobile phone
das hochauflösende Display	high-resolution display
der Klingelton (⁼e)	ring tone
die Medien (pl)	media
der Messenger-Dienst (-e)	messaging service
nachrüsten	to update
das Passwort (⁼er)	password, pass code
das Selfie (-s)	selfie
sprachgesteuert	hands-free
auf stumm schalten	to switch to silent
die Sucht (⁼e)	addiction
das Telefonat (-e)	phone call
die Telefongebühr (-en)	call charge
die Unterhaltung	entertainment
der Vertrag (⁼e)	contract
die Voicemail (-s)	voicemail

....

der Akku hält tagelang	the battery lasts for days
etw. per Handy einstellen	to switch sth. on from one's mobile
Fotografieren ist die am meisten genutzte Funktion	taking photos is the most used function
man hat alles in einem Gerät	you have everything in one device

---

Websites

You will find other useful articles, links and vocabulary on this topic on the following website:

www.bsi.bund.de *Federal Office for Internet Security*

Strategy

Noun genders

In the fast-changing world of digital communications, vocabulary is often adopted directly from English without change. The question is: what gender should the nouns have in German? This is usually taken from the closest German word, or from its ending. For example:

- **der** Computer (noun ends in -*er*)
- **die** Software (noun: *die Ware*)
- **das** Notebook (noun: *das Buch*)

New words appear in languages all the time; when you meet them, make a note of them, together with their gender and plural.

A   Welche Wörter sind Maskulinum, Femininum, Neutrum? Aus welchen deutschen Wörtern könnte man den jeweils dazugehörigen Artikel herausfinden?
1   Internet
2   Playlist
3   Smartphone
4   E-Mail
5   App
6   Livestream
7   Onlinebanking
8   Plattform
9   Selfie
10 SMS

Strategy

Recent German words (neologisms)

Some new German words borrowed from English have been adapted to the rules of German grammar. This is especially true of verbs. Note these carefully when you come across them.

B   Die folgenden Wörter sind (meistens!) aus dem Englischen übernommen; ihre grammatischen Formen haben sich jedoch leicht geändert. Notieren Sie ihre Bedeutungen sowie die geforderten Ableitungen.

1   einloggen (Partizip Perfekt)
2   downloaden (Partizip Perfekt)
3   mailen (Partizip Perfekt)
4   die Webseite (Plural)
5   simsen (Partizip Perfekt)
6   googeln (Partizip Perfekt)
7   tweeten (Partizip Perfekt)
8   das Handy (Plural)
9   der Troll (Plural)
10 der Follower (Plural)

3 Jugendkultur: Mode, Musik und Fernsehen

aktuell	current, up to date
sich (einen Film) anschauen	to watch a film
aussehen (ie-a-e)	to look, appear
das Aussehen	appearance
die Band (-s)	band, group
die Bekleidung	clothing
beliebt bei (+Dat)	popular with
sich entspannen	to relax
das Image	image
klassische Musik	classical music
die Kleider	clothes
die Klamotten (inf)	clothes
klingen (i-a-u)	to sound
sich (Dat) leisten können	to be able to afford
so was kann ich mir nicht leisten	I can't afford that sort of thing
die Markenkleidung	designer clothing
der Musiker (-)	musician
die Musikrichtung (-en)	music genre
das Programm (-e)	channel, programme guide
die Qualität	quality
der Sänger (-) / die Sängerin (-nen)	singer
das Selbstbewusstsein	confidence
die Sendung (-en)	broadcast, programme
der Song (-s) / das Lied (-er)	song
der Streamingdienst (-e)	streaming service
der Text (-e)	lyrics
unsicher	insecure
die Unterhaltung	entertainment
das Vorbild (-er)	role model
die Vor- und Nachteile	advantages and disadvantages

3.1 Mode und Image — *Fashion and image*

achten auf (+Acc)	to notice
angeberisch	pretentious
angesagt	fashionable, trendy
gut / schlecht angezogen	well / badly dressed
anhaben (irreg)	to be wearing

anprobieren	to try on
athletisch	athletic
sich ausdrücken	to express o.s.
sich ausgegrenzt fühlen	to feel excluded
die Baseballmütze (-n)	baseball cap
begehrenswert	desirable, attractive
heiß begehrt	highly sought-after
cool	cool
der Designer (-)	designer
fragwürdig	questionable
die Frisur (-en)	hair-style
seine Frisur stylen	to do one's hair
das Gemisch	mixture
der Geschmack (-̈e / -̈er)	taste
der Gruppenzwang	peer pressure
günstig	reasonable (in price)
hässlich	ugly
mit der Herde laufen* (ä-ie-au)	to follow the herd
der Herdentrieb	herd instinct
hübsch	pretty
das Individuum (pl Individuen)	individual
von Jahr zu Jahr	from year to year
der Kapuzenpullover (-)	hoodie
das Kleidungsstück (-e)	item of clothing
kurzlebig	short-lived
der Mode folgen*	to follow fashion
im Modebereich arbeiten	to work in the fashion industry
modebewusst	fashion-conscious
das Modebewusstsein	dress sense
der Modefreak (-s)	fashionista
das Modeheft (-e)	fashion magazine
der eigene Modestil	your own style
das Model (-s)	(fashion) model
das Muster (-)	pattern, design
jdn. nachahmen	to imitate s.o.
jdm. nacheifern	to emulate s.o.
oberflächlich	superficial
das Outfit (-s)	outfit
die Saison	season (in fashion)
schick	stylish
die Schuluniform (-en)	school uniform

sinnlos	pointless
der Stil (-e)	style
die Subkultur	sub-culture
sich tätowieren lassen (ä-ie-a)	to get a tattoo
die Tätowierung (-en)	tattoo
veralten* (*itr*)	to date (fashion)
verspotten	to mock
wegschmeißen (ei-i-i)	to throw away
zeitlos	timeless, classic
sich zurechtmachen	to get ready

....

ein Ausdruck der Individualität	an expression of individualism
ein Ausdruck von Zugehörigkeit	an expression of belonging
die aktuelle Mode	current fashion
in Mode / aus der Mode kommen* (o-a-o)	to come into / go out of fashion
nach der neuesten Mode gekleidet	dressed in the latest fashion
man wird ausgeschlossen	you're excluded
Was liegt heute im Trend?	What's cool just now?
durch die Läden schlendern	to stroll around the shops
in Ausbeuterbetrieben produzieren	to manufacture in sweatshops
alles dreht sich um das Aussehen	everything has to do with your appearance
alles geht	anything goes
Mode ist mir egal	I can't be bothered with fashion
ich halte Mode für oberflächlich	I think fashion is superficial
Charakter ist wichtiger als Aussehen	character is more important than appearance
man kann sich selbst in seiner Kleidung ausdrücken	you can express your personality by what you wear

Der Körper	***The body***
abnehmen / zunehmen (*irreg*)	to lose / put on weight
die Bewegung (-en)	movement, exercise
bewundern	to admire
eine Diät machen	to go on a diet
fettleibig	obese
das Fitnessstudio (-s)	fitness studio
gesund	healthy
sich gesund ernähren	to eat healthily
auf das Gewicht achten	to watch one's weight
der Lebensstil (-e)	life-style

die Magersucht	anorexia
magersüchtig	anorexic
das Make-up	make-up
das Modelmaß	model-like proportions
muskelbepackt	with bulging muscles
das Muskelpaket (-e)	six-pack
muskulös	muscular
der Neid / neidisch	envy / envious
der modellierte Oberkörper (-)	sculpted torso
sich richten nach	to conform to
so schlank sein* (irreg) wie …	to be as slim as…
schlapp	lethargic
sich schminken	to put on make-up
die Schönheitsoperation	cosmetic surgery
der Schönheitswahn	obsession with beauty
Sport treiben (ei-ie-ie)	to do sport
trainieren	to train
die Traumfigur	dream figure
übergewichtig	overweight
unzufrieden	dissatisfied
sich verwandeln in (+Acc)	to transform o.s. into

ich fühle mich in meiner Haut wohl	I feel good about myself
Modelfotos werden retuschiert	photos of models are touched up
eine ausgewogene Ernährung	a balanced diet
in Bezug auf die Körpergröße ein gesundes Gewicht haben (irreg)	to have a healthy weight in relation to one's body size
unterschiedliche Körperformen	different body shapes
einem Sportverein beitreten* (i-a-e)	to join a sports club
um mein Gewicht mache ich mir keine Sorgen (pl)	I don't worry about my weight
ein gesunder Geist in einem gesunden Körper	a healthy mind in a healthy body
Frischluft und Bewegung	fresh air and exercise
sich regelmäßig bewegen	to exercise regularly

3.2 Die Bedeutung der Musik für Jugendliche

The importance of music for young people

das Album (*pl* Alben)	album
auftreten* (i-a-e) (*itr*)	to perform, appear
der Auftritt (-e)	performance, gig
beeinflusst von (+*Dat*)	influenced by
die Begleitung	backing (e.g. vocals)
die Beliebtheit	popularity
der / das Download (-s)	download
downloadbar	downloadable
downloaden	to download
eintönig	monotonous
Erfolg haben (*irreg*)	to be successful
der Fan (-s)	fan
das Gefühl (-e)	feeling
die Hitparade	the charts
der Jazz	jazz
kitschig	kitschy, cheesy
Klavier / Geige spielen	to play the piano / violin
das Konzert (-e)	concert
der Leadsänger (-)	lead singer
live singen (i-a-u), spielen	to perform live
die Melodie (-n)	tune
misstönend	discordant
mitsingen (i-a-u)	to sing along
das Musical (-s)	musical
die Musikberieselung	constant background music
das Musikfestival (-s)	music festival
musizieren	to play a musical instrument
die Muttersprache (-n)	native language
der Ohrwurm (¨er)	catchy / unforgettable tune
der Plattenvertrag (¨e)	recording contract
die Playlist (-s)	playlist
rappen	to rap
die Raubkopie (-n)	pirated copy
der Rhythmus (*pl* Rhythmen)	rhythm
die Schallplatte (-n)	vinyl record
singen (i-a-u) über (+*Acc*)	to sing about
der Songschreiber (-)	songwriter
der Straßenmusikant (-en)	street musician, busker

der Takt	beat
der Text (-e)	lyrics
auf Tournee	on tour
üben	to practise
weltbekannt / weltberühmt	world-famous
werben (i-a-o) für (+Acc)	to promote
der Zuhörer (-)	listener

einen Streaming-Dienst abonnieren	to subscribe to a streaming service
die persönlichen Musikvorlieben	personal preferences in music
eine treue Fangemeinde haben (irreg)	to have a loyal fan base
verträumte Melodien	dreamy melodies
Musik als Hintergrund	music as a background
die sinkende Bereitschaft, für Musik zu bezahlen	the declining willingness to pay for music
Musik über YouTube hören	to listen to music on YouTube
in den Texten geht es um …	the lyrics are about…
alltägliche Sehnsüchte, Träume und Ängste	everyday longings, dreams and fears
es klingt nach / wie …	it sounds like…
die Musik sagt Jugendlichen zu	the music appeals to young people
es macht mir gute Laune	it puts me in a good mood
die neuesten Musiktrends	the latest trends in music

Klassische Musik	*Classical music*
aufführen (tr)	to perform
begleiten	to accompany
die Blechbläser (pl)	brass (section)
der Chor (¨-e)	choir
der Dirigent (-en)	conductor
die Emotion (-en)	emotion
der Flügel (-)	grand piano
die Holzbläser (pl)	woodwind (section)
das Kammerorchester (-)	chamber orchestra
die Kapelle (-n)	band (brass etc)
komponieren	to compose
der Komponist (-en)	composer
der Konzertsaal (pl -säle)	concert hall
musikalisch	musical
der Musikfreund (-e)	music-lover
das Musikstück (-e)	piece of music

die Noten (*pl*)	(sheet) music
die Oper (-n)	opera
das Orchester (-)	orchestra
die Partitur (-en)	score
probieren einstudieren	to rehearse
die Saite (-n)	string
das Schlagzeug	percussion (section)
der Solist (-en)	soloist
die Streicher (*pl*)	strings (section)
tiefsinning	profound
der Ton (-e)	note (sound)
der Virtuose (-n)	virtuoso

in einer Band spielen	to play in a band
im Chor singen	to sing in a choir
vom Blatt spielen	to sight-read
nach Gehör spielen	to play by ear
in ein Konzert gehen* (*irreg*)	to go to a concert
jdn. musikalisch ausbilden	to train s.o. in music
richtig / falsch singen	to sing in / out of tune
die zeitgenössische Musik	contemporary music
Übung macht den Meister	practice makes perfect

3.3 Die Rolle des Fernsehens *The role of television*

zur Ablenkung	for relaxation, as a distraction
die Abwechslung	variety, change
aktuell	current, up to date
der Alleinunterhalter (-) der Stand-up-Comedian (-s)	stand-up comedian
sich ausruhen	to relax
ausstrahlen	to broadcast
beeinflussen	to influence
bequem	comfortable
der Bewegungsmangel	lack of physical exercise
der Bildschirm (-e)	screen
dumm	stupid
einschalten / ausschalten	to switch on / switch off
zum Entspannen	for relaxation

die Fernbedienung (-en)	remote control
fernsehen (i-a-e) ⎫ Fernseh(en) gucken ⎭	to watch television
der Fernseher (-) ⎫ das Fernsehgerät (-e) ⎭	television set
der Fernsehkonsum	television consumption
das Fernsehprogramm (-e)	television schedule
gehirnamputiert (*inf*)	dead from the neck up (*inf*)
die Gewalt	violence
vor der Glotze sitzen (*irreg*) (*inf*)	to sit in front of the box (*inf*)
im Hintergrund laufen (ä-ie-au)	to be on in the background
sich informieren	to find out, inform o.s.
durch die Kanäle zappen	to flick through the channels
kindisch	childish
lächerlich	ridiculous
die Langeweile	boredom
sich über jdn. / etw. lustig machen	to make fun of s.o. / sth.
Nützliches erfahren (ä-u-a)	to learn useful things
oberflächlich	superficial
passiv	passive
peinlich	embarrassing
im Rampenlicht	in the spotlight
schaffen (a-u-a)	to create
das Second-screening	dual screening
seicht, trivial	trivial, shallow
spannend	exciting
täglich	daily
die unkritische Haltung	uncritical attitude
vegetieren ⎫ vertrotteln (*inf*) ⎭	to vegetate
verharmlosen	to make sth. appear harmless
wertlos	worthless
die Zeiteinteilung	how one uses one's time
eine reine Zeitverschwendung	just a waste of time
der Zuschauer (-)	viewer

....

Was kommt heute Abend im Fernsehen?	What's on television this evening?
mehrere Stunden pro Tag	several hours a day
er verwendet Computer und Fernseher immer gleichzeitig	he always watches television at the same time as he's using his computer

da kann man selbst bestimmen	you can decide for yourself
sich einen Film im Internet anschauen	to watch a film on the internet
man kann sich Filme anschauen, wann und wo man will	you can watch films whenever and wherever you want
das Fernsehen verliert an Bedeutung	television is becoming less important
darüber wird geschwärmt	people are really enthusiastic about it
es erweitert den Horizont	it broadens your horizons
die Macht des Internets	the power of the internet
man will das Fernsehen neu erfinden	they want to re-invent television
den Fernsehkonsum begrenzen	to limit television viewing
Eltern sollten verhindern, dass ihre Kinder…	parents should prevent their children from…

Der Rundfunk / *Broadcasting media*

der Actionfilm (-e)	action film
der Ansager (-)	announcer
aufnehmen (*irreg*) / aufzeichnen	to record
die Castingshow (-s)	talent show
der Dokumentarfilm (-e)	documentary
die Einschaltquoten	viewing figures
die Fernsehgebühren (*pl*)	television licence fee
die (Sende)folge (-n)	episode
das Heimkino (-s)	home cinema
hochauflösendes Fernsehen	high-definition television
der Hörfunk	radio
das Interview (-s)	interview
interviewen (*pf* hat … interviewt)	to interview
der Kassenschlager (-)	blockbuster
der Krimi (-s)	crime / detective film
die Kultur	culture
live (*invar*)	live
die Liveübertragung (-en)	live broadcast
der Moderator (-en)	presenter
die Nachricht / die Nachrichten (*pl*)	item of news / the news
die Nachrichtensendung (-en) / die Tagesschau	news programme
das öffentlich-rechtliche Fernsehen	public-service television
die Online-Videothek (-en)	online video library
das Reality-TV	reality TV

die Realityshow (-s) ⎤ die Containershow (-s) ⎦	reality TV show
die Seifenoper (-n)	soap opera
der Sender (-)	station / channel
die Serie (-n)	series
die Spielshow (-s)	game show
die Staffel (-n)	season, series
das Weltgeschehen	world events
der Werbeblock (¨e)	commercial break
der Werbespot (-s)	(television) ad
die Werbung	advertising
die Wettervorhersage (-n)	weather forecast
der Zeichentrickfilm (-e)	cartoon

....

„Sie hören die Nachrichten (*pl*)"	"Here is the news"
mit den Nachrichten auf dem Laufenden bleiben* (ei-ie-ie)	to keep up to date with the news
wie soeben gemeldet wird, ...	according to reports just coming in…
Livesendungen lassen den Zuschauer am aktuellen Geschehen teilhaben	live broadcasts allow viewers to keep up with events as they happen
sich durch Werbeeinnahmen (*pl*) finanzieren	to be financed by advertising revenue
der Kampf um Zuschauer	the ratings battle

Websites

You will find other useful articles, links and vocabulary on this topic on the following website:

www.bpb.de/gesellschaft/kultur/jugendkulturen-in-deutschland/ (https://tinyurl.com/ybcz9oyo)

Strategy

Compound nouns: genders

German is famous for its compound nouns, i.e. consisting of several elements – usually no more than three, though it is possible to form much longer words, usually as a joke. But long German words are always made up of shorter German words. When you meet an unfamiliar compound noun, always look first at the last element:

● the last element will tell you what the word is about
● the gender and plural of the last element will be the gender and plural for the whole word

A Unterstreichen Sie das letzte Element in diesen zusammengesetzten Substantiven, und bestimmen Sie den Artikel (*der, die, das*).

1 Streamingdienst
2 Nachteil
3 Modebereich
4 Modebewusstsein
5 Lebensstil
6 Schönheitswahn
7 Schönheitsoperation
8 Körpergröße
9 Musikfestival
10 Songschreiber

Strategy

Compound nouns: formation

The first elements of compound nouns can be almost any parts of speech – with each new noun encountered, work out whether this is an adjective, an adverb (more rarely), a preposition, or a verb-stem. (Compound nouns whose first element is a noun are dealt with on p. 85.)

B Sagen Sie, aus welchen Wortarten jedes Substantiv besteht – Adjektiv / Adverb / Präposition / Verbstamm + Substantiv.

1 der Hintergrund
2 der Zuschauer
3 die Einschaltquoten
4 der Hörfunk
5 der Werbespot
6 die Unterhaltung
7 das Vorbild
8 die Magersucht
9 die Langeweile
10 die Fernbedienung

Theme 2 — Artistic culture in the German-speaking world

4 Feste und Traditionen

der Anfang (⁀e)	start
sich ausruhen	to rest, relax
bieten (ie-o-o)	to offer, give
die Blume (-n)	flower
der Brauch (⁀e)	custom
Bräuche und Sitten (*pl*)	customs and traditions
christlich	Christian (*adj*)
einladen (ä-u-a)	to invite
das Ende	end
essen (i-a-e)	to eat
evangelisch	Protestant (*adj*)
die Feier (-n)	party
die Feierlichkeiten	festivities
feiern	to celebrate
der Feiertag (-e)	public holiday
das Fest (-e)	celebration
sich freuen auf (+*Acc*)	to look forward to
der Gast (⁀e)	guest
das Geschenk (-e)	present, gift
gesellig	sociable
glauben an (+*Acc*)	to believe in
der Höhepunkt (-e)	climax
die Jahreszeit (-en)	season
katholisch	Catholic (*adj*)
lebendig	alive / lively
die Religion (-en)	religion
schmücken	to decorate
die Schokolade	chocolate
der Spaß	fun
der Ursprung (⁀e)	origin
die Verwandten (*adj.noun pl*)	relatives
vorbei sein* (*irreg*)	to be over, past
die Vorbereitung (-en)	preparation

4.1 Feste und Traditionen – ihre Wurzeln und Ursprünge

Festivals and traditions – their roots and origins

sich ableiten von (+*Dat*)	to be derived from
abschrecken	to scare away
sich ändern	to change
der Anlass (¨e)	cause, reason
anzünden	to light
das Bedürfnis (-se)	need
beharrlich	unchanging, persistent
beliebt	much-loved, popular
der Bestandteil (-e)	part
der Bettler (-)	beggar
die Birke (-n)	birch-tree
böse / das Böse	evil (*adj*) / evil (*noun*)
das Brauchtum	customs and traditions
der Brunnen (-)	fountain
das Christentum	Christianity
sich durchsetzen	to become generally accepted, catch on
der Einfluss (¨e)	influence
entstehen* (*irreg*)	to arise, originate from
sich entwickeln	to develop
erschrecken (*tr*)	to frighten
erzeugen	to produce
der Geist (-er)	spirit
die Gemeinde (-n)	community, local authority
die Geselligkeit	sociability
die Grundlage (-n)	basis
der Handwerker (-)	craftsman
heidnisch	pagan
die Heimat	home town, region, country
die Hexe (-n)	witch
der Höhepunkt (-e)	highlight
der Kampf (¨e)	fight, battle
die Kerze (-n)	candle
der König (-e) / die Königin (-nen)	king / queen
locken	to tempt
in der Nacht	at night, during the night
der Narr (-en)	fool, jester

prägen	to influence, characterise
das Ritual (-e)	ritual
das Schaltjahr (-e)	leap year
schätzen	to value
schmücken	to decorate
die Sonnenwende	solstice
stammen aus (+Dat)	to originate in, stem from
der Streich (-e)	practical joke
der Teufel (-)	devil
typisch für (+Acc)	typical of
der Umzug (¨e)	procession
ursprünglich	original (adj)
verhüllen	to mask, cover
sich verkleiden	to dress up, disguise o.s.
die Verlässlichkeit	dependability
verschmelzen (i-o-o)	to merge, fuse
vertraut	familiar
der Vorabend	the evening before
vorchristlich	pre-Christian
die Weihnachtskugel (-n)	bauble
widmen (+Dat)	to dedicate
die Wurzel (-n)	root
die Verwurzelung	rootedness
das Zeichen (-)	sign, badge
zittern	to tremble

lebendiges Brauchtum	living tradition
die emotionale Bindung an (+Acc)	the emotional bond with
ein Symbol für …	a symbol of…
das Zugehörigkeitsgefühl	the sense of belonging
über Jahrhunderte hinweg	through the centuries
von alters her	since time immemorial
sie haben religiöse Grundlagen (pl)	they have a religious basis
sie vermitteln ein Gefühl von …	they give a feeling of…
sie geben dem Menschen Halt	they give support to people
… existiert seit …	…has existed for / since…
Traditionen pflegen	to maintain traditions
… verliert an Bedeutung	…is declining in significance
die Ursprünge liegen im Dunkel der Vergangenheit	the origins are lost in the mists of time

Weihnachten	*Christmas*
der Adventskalender (-)	advent calendar
der Adventskranz (⁼e)	advent wreath
die Adventszeit	Advent
das Ambiente	ambience, atmosphere
aufgeregt sein über (+Acc)	to get excited about
aufmachen	to open
aufwachen* (itr)	to wake up
wecken (tr)	to wake s.o. up
backen (ä-a-a)	to bake
die Bescherung	the giving of presents
beten, das Gebet (-e)	to pray, prayer
bunte Lichter	fairy lights
das Christkind	the Christ-child
der Christstollen (-)	Christmas cake
die Dekorationen	decorations
das Dreikönigsfest	Epiphany (6 Jan)
der Engel (-)	angel
das Festessen	celebration meal
die Feuerzangenbowle (-n)	red wine punch with rum
die Gans (⁼e)	goose
die Geburt (-en)	birth
es geht um (+Acc)	it's about…
gemütlich	snug, cosy
die Glaskugel (-n)	glass tree bauble
das Glockengeläut	the ringing of bells
der Glühwein	mulled wine
der Heiligabend	Christmas Eve (24 Dec)
am Heiligabend	on Christmas Eve
der Imbissstand (⁼e)	food stall
die Kerze (-n)	candle
die Kerzen anzünden	to light the candles
in die Kirche gehen* (irreg)	to go to church
die Krippe (-n)	crib (for nativity)
der Lebkuchen (-)	soft spicy biscuit
die Mandel (-n) / gebrannte Mandeln	almond / roasted almonds
die Marktbude (-n)	market stall
die Marone (-n)	chestnut
die Messe (-n)	church service
der Gottesdienst (-e)	

der Nikolaustag	St. Nicholas' Day (6 Dec)
öffentlich	public
das Plätzchen (-)	biscuit
die Pralinen	chocolates
schätzen	to value, treasure
das Schaufenster (-)	shop windows
jdm. etw. schenken	to give s.o. sth. (as a present)
selbst gemacht	home-made
der (Verkaufs)stand (¨e)	market stall
die Sternsinger	carol singers (6 Jan in Germany)
sich streiten (ei-i-i) mit (+Dat)	to argue with
der Tannenbaum (¨e)	fir tree
vertraut	familiar
weihnachtlich (adj)	Christmassy
der Weihnachtsbaum (¨e)	Christmas tree
das Weihnachtsgebäck	Christmas biscuits
die Weihnachtskarte (-n)	Christmas card
das Weihnachtslied (-er)	Christmas carol
der Weihnachtsmann	Father Christmas (6 Dec)
der Weihnachtsmarkt (¨e)	Christmas market
der erste Weihnachtstag	Christmas Day (25 Dec)
der zweite Weihnachtstag	Boxing Day (26 Dec)
die Wintersonnenwende	winter solstice
sich (Dat) etw. wünschen	to wish for sth. (as gift)

Frohe Weihnachten!	Happy Christmas!
zu Weihnachten	at Christmas
auf den Weihnachtsmarkt gehen* (irreg)	to go to the Christmas market
wir legen viel Wert auf …	we set a lot of store by…
eine besinnliche Zeit	a quiet, thoughtful time
auf der ganzen Welt	all over the world
die Tradition wird groß geschrieben	tradition is really important
alte Bräuche pflegen	to maintain old traditions
man liest aus der Bibel vor	we read from the Bible
wir feiern die Geburt Jesu Christi	we celebrate the birth of Christ
etw. gebührend feiern	to celebrate sth. properly
… gehören dazu	…are part of it
die Kirchenglocken läuten	the church-bells ring

Silvester und Neujahr	*New Year's Eve / Day*
beliebt	popular
Blei gießen (ie-o-o)	*telling fortunes by shapes formed by molten metal dropped into water*
fernsehen (ie-a-e)	to watch television
das Feuerwerk	fireworks
um Mitternacht	at midnight
das Neujahr, an Neujahr	New Year, at New Year
„Prosit!" / „Zum Wohl!"	"Cheers!" / "To your health!"
„Prosit Neujahr!"	"Here's to the New Year!"
schmelzen* (i-o-o)	to melt
der Sekt	Champagne, sparkling wine
die Silvesterparty (-s)	New Year's Eve party
teilnehmen (*irreg*) an (+*Dat*)	to take part in
der Teilnehmer (-)	participant
der Vorsatz (⁻e)	resolution

man lässt das vergangene Jahr Revue passieren	people look back over the old year
das Neujahr begrüßen	to see in the New Year
in die Zukunft schauen, blicken	to look into the future
die Zukunft vorraussagen	to predict the future
Ein glückliches neues Jahr! ⎫ Guten Rutsch! ⎭	Happy New Year!
ein (guter) Vorsatz für das neue Jahr	New Year's resolution
man stößt auf (+/Acc/) ... an	we raise a glass to…
man zählt die letzten Sekunden des alten Jahres laut herunter	people count down the last seconds of the old year aloud
zu einem Ritual werden* (i-u-o)	to become a tradition
man wünscht sich Glück	we wish one another happiness

Ostern	*Easter*
das Abendmahl	communion, eucharist (church service)
Aschermittwoch	Ash Wednesday
die Fastenzeit (-en)	Lent, time of fasting
Fastnachtsdienstag	Shrove Tuesday
die Fruchtbarkeit	fertility
der Frühling	spring
gedenken (*irreg*) (+*Gen*)	to remember, think about

der Gläubige (*adj. noun*)	believer
Gründonnerstag	Maundy Thursday
der Karfreitag	Good Friday
die Kirchenglocke (-n)	church bell
das Kreuz (-e)	cross
die Kreuzigung	crucifixion
der Lammbraten	roast lamb
läuten	to sound, ring
das Osterei (-er)	Easter egg
der Osterhase (-n)	Easter bunny (*lit.* hare)
die Osterglocke (-n) ⎫ die Narzisse (-n) ⎭	daffodil
das Ostern	Easter
zu Ostern	at Easter
Ostersonntag	Easter Sunday
Pfingsten	Whitsun, Pentecost
Rosenmontag	Carnival Monday
das Schokoladenei (-er)	chocolate egg
der Tod	death
verzichten auf (+*Acc*)	to go without, give up

die Kreuzigung und Auferstehung Christi	the crucifixion and resurrection of Christ
„Jesus ist auferstanden!"	"Christ is risen!"

Jüdische und islamische Feiern   *Jewish and Islamic celebrations*

der Fastenmonat (-e)	month of fasting
der Koran	Koran
die Moschee (-n)	mosque
das Pessach	Passover
der Ramadan	Ramadan
der Rosch ha-Schana	Jewish New Year
die Süßigkeit (-en)	sweet
die Synagoge (-n)	synagogue
verteilen	to hand out
verzeihen (ei-ie-ie)	to forgive
das Zuckerfest	end of Ramadan

4.2 Feste und Traditionen – ihre soziale und wirtschaftliche Bedeutung heute

Festivals and traditions – their social and economic importance today

das Angebot (-e)	supply, offer
anstellen / einstellen	to employ
der Auftrag (-̈e)	commission, order
ausgelassen	lively, boisterous
ausschenken	to pour (out), serve
aussterben* (i-a-o)	to die out
bedeuten	to mean
die Bedeutung (-en)	significance, importance
der Beitrag (-̈e)	contribution
beitragen (ä-u-a) zu (+Dat)	to contribute to
sich beteiligen an (+Dat)	to take part in
betragen (ä-u-a)	to amount to (money)
das Einkommen (-)	income
das Ereignis (-se)	event, occurrence
erheblich	considerable
der Erlös (-e)	proceeds
fröhlich / die Fröhlichkeit	merry / merriness
der Gast (-̈e)	guest
die Gaststätte (-n)	restaurant, pub
das Gaststättengewerbe	catering trade
das Gedränge	crowd, crush
der Geldbeutel (-)	purse, wallet
der Gemeinschaftssinn	sense of community
das Gewerbe (-)	trade
der Gewinn (-e)	profit
Gewinn erzielen	to make a profit
der Händler (-)	shop-keeper, dealer
herstellen / der Hersteller (-)	to produce / producer
karitativ	charitable
die Kaufkraft	spending power (of customer)
die Kauflust / kauflustig	desire to buy / in a spending mood
der Kaufrausch	spending spree
kaufsüchtig sein* (irreg)	to be a shopaholic
kitschig / der Kitsch	kitschy (garish) / kitsch

kommerzialisiert	commercialised
das Kulturerbe	cultural heritage
der Materialismus	materialism
das Merkmal (-e)	characterisitic, feature
die Nachfrage	demand
der Obdachlose (*adj. noun*)	homeless person
saufen	to drink (heavily)
jdm. etw. schenken	to give s.o. sth.
im Schlussverkauf	in the sales
das Sonderangebot (-e)	special offer
spenden	to donate
stärken	to reinforce, strengthen
tauschen	to exchange
die Übernachtung (-en)	overnight stay
der Umsatz	turnover
der Unternehmer (-)	businessman
unterstützen (*insep*)	to support
veranstalten	to organise
die Veranstaltung (-en)	event
verschwenden	to waste
die Versuchung	temptation
die Ware (-n)	product (*pl* goods, merchandise)
wesentlich	essential
das Wesentliche	the essential thing
wirtschaftlich	economic
der Wunschzettel (-)	wish-list
die Zahl (-en)	figure, number

das Einkaufen im Internet	online shopping
tief in den Geldbeutel greifen (ei-i-i)	to dig deep (financially)
den Gürtel enger schnallen	to tighten one's belt
ich hatte ein bisschen zu viel des Guten	I ate and drank a bit too much
etw. in Geschenkpapier einwickeln	to gift-wrap sth.
wir geben zu viel Geld aus	we spend too much money
Überflüssiges kaufen / verschenken	to buy / give stuff that's not needed
es wird hektischer, lauter, stressiger	it gets more hectic, louder and more stressful
ich konnte der Versuchung nicht widerstehen	I couldn't resist the temptation

4.3 Vielfältige Feste und Traditionen in verschiedenen Regionen

The diversity of festivities and traditions in different regions

albern	silly, ridiculous
jdm. Angst machen	to frighten s.o.
sich anziehen (*irreg*)	to dress
aussterben* (i-a-o)	to die out
der Ball (⁼e)	ball, party
der Bauer (-n) / die Bäuerin (-nen)	farmer / farmer's wife
bedrohen	to threaten
der Besen (-)	broom
sich betrinken (i-a-u)	to get drunk
die Blaskapelle (-n)	brass band
das Bundesland (⁼er)	federal state
bundesweit / landesweit	nationwide / in a particular federal state
bunt geschmückt	colourfully decorated
der Bürgermeister (-)	mayor
Dampf ablassen (ä-ie-a)	to let off steam
das Dirndl (-)	women's dress in S. Germany, Austria
einzigartig	unique
entstehen* (*irreg*)	to originate
die Ernte (-n)	harvest
das Erntedankfest (-e)	harvest festival
die Eröffnungsfeier (-n)	opening ceremony
die Folklore	folk music, folklore
Fronleichnam	Corpus Christi
der Gaukler (-)	travelling entertainer
gelten (i-a-o) als	to be considered to be
das Geräusch (-e)	sound, noise
der gesetzliche Feiertag (-e)	national holiday
die Heckenwirtschaft (-en) / die Besenwirtschaft (-en) / die Straußwirtschaft (-en)	*seasonal pub run by wine-growers (marked by broom or bunches of flowers)*
herumalbern	to fool around
der Hintergrund (⁼e)	background
der Jahrestag (-e)	anniversary
Karneval / Fastnacht / Fasching	Carnival
der Karnevalszug (⁼e)	Carnival procession
die Kirmes (-sen)	fun-fair
der Klang (⁼e)	(musical) sound

das Kostüm (-e)	fancy dress
der Krach	din, racket
die Kuhglocke (-n)	cow-bell
der Lärm	(loud) noise
die Luftschlange (-n)	streamer
die Maske (-n)	mask
der Maßkrug (¨e)	beer stein (*litre*)
der Narr (-en)	fool, jester
der Partylöwe (-n)	party animal
die Passionsspiele (*pl*)	Passion Play
der Polterabend	pre-wedding party
eine Rede halten (ä-ie-a)	to make a speech
das Richtfest (-e)	topping-out party (*new building*)
das Schaltjahr (-e)	leap year
das Schützenfest (-e)	fair with marksmen's competition
der Schützenkönig (-e)	best marksman
stattfinden (i-a-u)	to take place
die Stimmung (-en)	mood
stolz auf (+*Acc*)	proud of
der Straßenmusikant (-en)	street musician
der Tag der deutschen Einheit	German Unity Day (3 Oct)
das Tal (¨er)	valley
tosend	thunderous (noise)
die Tracht (-en)	folk costume
das Trachtenfest (-e)	*festival where traditional costume is worn*
der Umzug (¨e)	procession
veranstalten	to put on (event)
die Veranstaltung (-en)	event
sich verkleiden	to disguise o.s. / wear fancy dress
verscheuchen	to scare away
vertreiben (ei-ie-ie)	to drive out, away
das Vieh	cattle
das Volksfest (-e)	festival, fair
der Volkstrauertag (-e)	Remembrance Sunday (two Sundays before Advent)
vorbei sein* (*irreg*)	to be over, past
das Wachstum	growth
der (Fest)wagen (-)	(carnival) float
die Weiberfastnacht	women's Carnival day
das Weinfest (-e)	wine festival

ziehen* (*irreg*) (*itr*)	to march, move, process
zuschauen	to look on

im Norden / Süden Deutschlands	in northern / southern Germany
in Norddeutschland / in Süddeutschland	in the north / south of Germany
in ganz Deutschland	all over Germany
Feuerwerke abbrennen (e-a-a)	to let off fireworks
an der Straße stehen (*irreg*)	to stand on the road-side
durch die Straßen ziehen* (*irreg*)	to process along the streets
viel Lärm machen	to make a huge racket
die bösen Geister vertreiben	to drive away evil spirits
durch etw. geprägt sein (*irreg*)	characterised by
wie ein Loch saufen (*inf*)	to drink like a fish
einen Maibaum aufstellen	to erect a May-pole
das närrische Treiben	carnival celebrations
in Partylaune	in a party mood
Rollen tauschen	to swap roles
das gilt als typisch deutsch	that's seen as typically German
bunte Lampions	colourful lights
die Tradition unterscheidet sich von Region zu Region	the tradition varies from one region to another
neue Freundschaften schließen (ie-o-o)	to make new friends
bei Einbruch der Dunkelheit	as night falls
bei Sonnenaufgang	as the sun rises

Websites

You will find other useful articles, links and vocabulary on this topic on the following websites:

**www.goruma.de/Laender/Europa/Deutschland/Wissenswertes/
Feiertage_Feste_und_Veranstaltungen.html
(https://tinyurl.com/y9t9ypz8)**

www.deutsche-lebensart.de

Strategy

Noun plurals

When you learn a new noun, always learn it with its gender and plural. Plurals are fairly predictable:

● **Masculine** nouns usually add **-e** or **⁻e**
● **Feminine** nouns usually add **-n** or **-en**
● **Neuter** nouns usually add **-e** or **-er** (with an umlaut if possible)

A Suchen Sie die Pluralformen zu folgenden Substantiven.
1 der Anfang
2 der Brauch
3 der Höhepunkt
4 die Hexe
5 die Zeit
6 die Rede
7 das Gebet
8 das Lied
9 das Band
10 das Tal

Strategy

Less expected noun plurals

While the patterns above apply to most nouns, there are of course exceptions. Once again, note them carefully as and when you encounter them and learn them and the gender together with the noun – vocabulary is always learned one word at a time, and patience is required!

B In der Liste unten finden Sie mehrere regelmäßige (aber auch ein paar unregelmäßige) Pluralformen. Notieren Sie sie!
1 der König
2 der Geist
3 der Kuchen
4 die Nacht
5 die Königin
6 die Zahl
7 die Stadt
8 das Geschenk
9 das Ereignis
10 das Märchen

5 Kunst und Architektur

der Architekt (-en)	architect
die Architektur / die Baukunst	architecture
ausdrücken	to express
die Ausstellung (-en)	exhibition
bauen / erbauen	to build
bedeutend	significant
das Bild (-er)	picture
darstellen	to depict, show
der Einfluss (¨e) / beeinflussen	influence / to influence
einzigartig	unique
entwerfen (i-a-o)	to design
die Farbe (-n)	colour, paint
das Gebäude (-)	building
die Gegenwart	the present
das Gemälde (-)	painting (object)
genießen (ie-o-o)	to enjoy
hervorragend	outstanding
das Jahrhundert (-e)	century
kultiviert	cultured
die Kunst	art
die Kunstgalerie (-n)	art gallery
der Künstler (-)	artist
künstlerisch	artistic
das Kunstwerk (-e)	work of art
malen / der Maler (-)	to paint / painter
die Malerei	painting (art form)
das Meisterwerk (-e)	masterpiece
renommiert	renowned
die Stilrichtung (-en)	style, trend
die Stimmung (-en)	atmosphere, mood
stimmungsvoll	atmospheric
die Vergangenheit	the past
wichtig	important
zeichnen	to draw
das Zeitalter (-)	age, period
die Zukunft	the future

5.1 Künstler und Architekten   *Artists and architects*

ablehnen	to reject
angewandte Kunst	applied art
die Anregung (-en)	inspiration
der Anspruch ("-e)	demand, requirement
das Atelier (-s)	studio, workshop
die Bauweise	construction method
begabt	gifted, talented
die Begabung (-en)	gift, talent
sich begeistern für (+Acc)	to be enthusiastic about
der Begriff (-e)	concept, term
die Bewegung (-en)	movement
die bildenden Künste	the fine arts
der Bildhauer (-)	sculptor
entwickeln (*tr*), sich entwickeln (*itr*)	to develop
experimentieren	to experiment
faszinieren	to fascinate
fertigstellen	to complete
der Gegensatz ("-e)	opposite, contrast
der Geist (-er)	mind, spirit
gelten (i-a-o) als	to be considered as
der Grafiker (-)	graphic artist
gründen	to found
das Hauptwerk (-e)	major work
der Höhepunkt (-e)	high point, peak
der Kontrast (-e)	contrast
die Kunstgeschichte	history of art
das Kunstgewerbe	arts and crafts
die Kunsthochschule (-n)	art college
die Kunstrichtung (-en)	trend or direction in art
malerisch	picturesque
prägen	to shape, mould
schaffen (a-u-a)	to create
die Skulptur (-en)	sculpture (art form)
der Ursprung ("-e)	origin
ursprünglich	originally
vielseitig	versatile, multi-talented
die Vorstellungskraft ⎱ die Fantasie ⎰	imagination

sich etw. (*+Dat*) widmen	to dedicate o.s. to
zählen zu (*+Dat*)	to be counted among

sie wurde von … beeinflusst	she was influenced by…
… ist im Museum zu sehen	…may be seen in the museum
er gilt als einer der größten …	he's considered to be one of the greatest…
abstrakte Kunst	abstract art
figurative / gegenständliche Kunst	figurative art
nach dem Leben zeichnen	to draw from life
sich malen lassen (ä-ie-a)	to have one's portrait painted
einen Beitrag leisten zu (*+Dat*)	to make a contribution to
die abendländische / morgenländische Kunst	Western / Oriental art

Ein Gemälde beschreiben	***Describing a painting***
abstrakt	abstract
der Akt (-e)	nude (depiction of)
das Aquarell (-e)	water-colour (painting)
beeindruckend	impressive
beschmieren	to daub (canvas)
drucken, der Druck (-e)	to print, print (artwork)
der Eindruck (¨e)	impression
empfinden (i-a-u)	to feel, sense
die Form (-en)	form, shape
gekennzeichnet durch (*+Acc*)	indicated by, shown by
geometrische Formen	geometric shapes
im Hintergrund / im Vordergrund	in the background / foreground
kitschig	trashy, posing as art
kritzeln / das Gekritzel	to doodle / doodling
die Landschaft (-en)	landscape
die Landschaftsmalerei	landscape painting
die Leinwand	canvas (material)
der Malstil (-e)	style of painting
das Merkmal (-e)	feature
das Modell (-e)	(artist's) model
Modell stehen (*irreg*)	to pose (for art-work)
das Motiv (-e)	subject (of e.g. a painting)
das Ölgemälde (-)	oil painting
das Original (-e)	original
die Palette (-n)	palette

der Pinsel (-)	brush
der Pinselstrich (-e)	brush-stroke
das Porträt (-s)	portrait
jdn. porträtieren	to paint a portrait of s.o.
das Selbstbildnis (-se)	self-portrait
skizzieren / die Skizze (-n)	to sketch / sketch
das Stillleben (-)	still-life
symbolisieren	to symbolise
die Zeichnung (-en)	drawing
zeigen	to show

Eine Skulptur beschreiben — *Describing a sculpture*

glatt	smooth
hauen	to sculpt
lebensecht	life-like
lebensgroß	life-size
aus Marmor	made of marble
plastisch	sculptural, three-dimensional
rau	rough
die Skulptur (-en) / die Plastik (-en)	sculpture (object)
der Sockel (-)	base, pedestal
die Statue (-n) / das Standbild (-er)	statue

Ein Gebäude beschreiben — *Describing a building*

architektonisch	architectural
der Backstein (-e)	brick
der Bau (pl Bauten)	construction, building
das Baumaterial (-ien)	building material
der Baustil (-e)	architectural style
bautechnisch	structural
die Bauweise	method of construction
das Bauwerk (-e)	building, edifice
der Beton	concrete
der Bogen (-)	arch
das Dach (¨er)	roof
im Erdgeschoss	on the ground floor
errichten / die Errichtung	to construct / construction
die Fassade (-n)	façade
das Fundament (-e)	foundation
geradlinig	straight

harmonisch	harmonious
die Innenarchitektur	interior design
die Innenausstattung	interior décor
kennzeichnen	to characterise
die Mauer (-n)	wall (exterior)
das Möbel (-)	piece of furniture / (pl) furniture
der Raum (¨e)	room / space
räumlich	spatial
rechteckig	rectangular
schätzen	to appreciate, value
das Stockwerk (-e)	storey
die Technik	technology
unterirdisch	underground
vereinfacht	simplified
verknüpfen	to link, connect
viereckig / quadratisch	square
die Wand (¨e)	wall (interior)
zweckmäßig	functional

einen Auftrag erhalten (ä-ie-a)	to receive a commission
ist durch (+Acc) ... geprägt	is characterised by…
es wirkt hell	it feels light
aus Glas, Stahl und Stein	made of glass, steel and stone

5.2 Kunst und Architektur im Alltag   *Art and architecture in everyday life*

abbilden	to illustrate, portray
die Abbildung (-en)	illustration, picture
angenehm	pleasant
sich anpassen (+Dat)	to adapt o.s. (to), to conform
die Aufnahme (-n)	photograph
sich auswirken auf (+Acc)	to have an effect on
die Auswirkung (-en)	effect
die Baustelle (-n)	building site
der Betonbunker (-)	ugly concrete building
der Betonklotz (¨e)	concrete block
das Bürohochhaus (¨er)	high-rise office block
emporragen über (+Acc)	to tower over

der Entwurf (⁻e)	design
der Fotoapparat (-e)	camera
der Fotograf (-en)	photographer
die Fotografie (-n)	photo / Photography (art form)
fotografieren	to photograph
das Graffiti (-s)	graffiti
großräumig	spacious, roomy
die Grünfläche (-n)	green space (in city)
hell / dunkel	light (well-lit) / dark
knipsen (*inf*)	to photograph
die Kopie (-n)	copy
der Kunstgegenstand (⁻e)	art object
das Objektiv (-e)	camera lens
öffentlich / privat	public / private
prägen	to mark, characterise
die Spraydose (-n)	spray can
das Stadtbild (-er)	town features, cityscape
ständig	permanent(ly), constant(ly)

das leibliche / geistige Wohl	physical / mental well-being
natürlich beleuchtet	lit by natural light
künstlerische Tätigkeiten	artistic activities
das künstlerische Angebot	what's on offer for art
ein Bild an die Wand hängen	to hang a picture on the wall
das Bild hängt an der Wand	the picture's hanging on the wall

5.3 Kunst und Architektur – Vergangenheit, Gegenwart, Zukunft

Art and architecture – past, present, future

Die Vergangenheit	***The past***
die Altstadt (⁻e)	old part of town
die Anfangsjahre	early years
der Auftrag (⁻e)	commission
das Baudenkmal (⁻er)	historical monument
beschädigt	damaged
sich beteiligen an (+*Dat*)	to participate in
die Blütezeit	heyday
das Denkmal (⁻er)	monument
erfinden (i-a-u)	to invent

das Fachwerkgebäude (-)	half-timbered building
mit etw. fertig werden* (i-u-o)	to come to terms with sth.
die Kuppel (-n)	dome, cupola
der Luftangriff (-e)	air raid
märchenhaft	fairy-tale
das Mittelalter	Middle Ages
mittelalterlich	medieval
prunkvoll	ostentatious
die Romanik	Romanesque (Norman) period
romanisch	Romanesque (Norman)
römisch	Roman
das römische Reich	Roman Empire
die Säule (-n)	column
das Schloss (¨er)	castle, stately home
die Stadtmauer (-n)	town wall
die Trümmer (*pl*)	ruins, rubble
der Turm (¨e)	tower
die Überreste	remains
unterdrücken (*insep*)	to suppress
das Vorbild (-er)	model
das Weltkulturerbe	world heritage site
wertvoll	valuable
wiederaufbauen	to rebuild
zerstören	to destroy

die meisten Leute	most people, the majority of people
X diente als Vorbild für ...	...was modelled on X
die damalige Technik	the technology of that time
es steht unter Denkmalschutz	it's a listed building
die Deutsche Stiftung Denkmalschutz	(= National Trust)
um die Jahrhundertwende	around the turn of the century
bis zum Ende des 20. Jahrhunderts	until the end of the 20th century
von (1939) bis (1945)	from (1939) to (1945)
dem Erdboden gleichmachen	to level to the ground
gut erhalten	well-preserved
das kulturelle Erbe	cultural heritage
in Schutt und Asche liegen	to lie in ruins
in den sechziger Jahren	in the 1960s
in großem Stil	on a magnificent scale

Gegenwart und Zukunft	*Present and future*
abreißen (ei-i-i)	to knock down
barrierefrei	open access (e.g. for disabled)
die Bauarbeiten	building works
der Bauboom (-s)	building boom
der Baumarkt (-̈e)	DIY store
die Bauweise	building method
das Bedürfnis (-se)	need, requirement
belebt	busy
beschränken	to limit
beseitigen	to remove
bestehen (*irreg*) aus (+*Dat*)	to consist of, be made of
bewahren	to preserve
sich eignen für (+*Acc*)	to be suitable for
der Energiebedarf	energy requirements
die Energieeffizienz	energy efficiency
der Energieverbrauch	energy consumption
erfinden (i-a-u)	to invent
die Fläche (-n)	piece of ground, area
gegenwärtig	of today, modern
die Heizung	heating
das Hochhaus (-̈er)	high-rise building
die Isolierung	insulation
klobig wirken	to look big and clumsy
kostengünstig	reasonably priced
leiden (*irreg*) unter (+*Dat*)	to suffer from
sich (*Dat*) etw. leisten	to afford
nachhaltig	sustainable
die Nachhaltigkeit	sustainability
ökologisch	ecological
das Passivhaus (-̈er)	energy-efficient building
der Pendelverkehr	commuter traffic
recyceln	to recycle
restaurieren	to renovate, restore
richtungsweisend	trend-setting
sanieren	to renovate / redevelop
schaden (+*Dat*)	to damage
die Siedlung (-en)	housing estate
die Solaranlage (-n)	solar installation
der Städteplaner (-)	town planner

das Stadtviertel (-)	district of town
die Tiefgarage (-n)	underground car-park
umgestalten	to remodel
verkehrsreich	busy (with traffic)
die Verkehrsverbindungen	transport connections (roads, rail etc.)
verwirklichen	to realise, put into action
das Wohnkonzept (-e)	concept for living, housing
der Wohnungsmangel	housing shortage
das Wohnviertel (-) } das Wohngebiet (-e)	residential area
zeitgemäß	in keeping with a particular time
der Zeitgenosse (-n)	contemporary (*noun*)
zeitgenössisch	contemporary (*adj*)
zukunftsweisend	forward-looking

dicht besiedelt	densely populated
in Einklang bringen (*irreg*) mit	to reconcile, harmonise with
die alternde Gesellschaft	the ageing society
einer Herausforderung genügen	to meet a challenge
Probleme bewältigen	to overcome problems
den Pkw-Verkehr aus der Innenstadt fernhalten	to ban cars from the town centre
auf den Menschen zugeschnitten	designed on a human scale

Websites

You will find other useful articles, links and vocabulary on this topic on the following website:

http://de.wikipedia.org/wiki/Kultur_Deutschlands

Strategy

Word families

As seen in Theme 1, Topic 1 (Activities), complex words are based on 'root' words or elements. When you come across an important word, spend some time with a dictionary discovering what other words are in the same family, initially with different parts of speech.

A Füllen Sie die Tabelle aus; Sie finden vielleicht mehrere Möglichkeiten.

	Verb	Substantiv	Person	Adjektiv/Adverb
1		die Architektur	....	....
2	malen	....	....	....
3		....	der/die Künstler/in	....
4	....	das Bild	....	....
5	....	das Foto	....	....
6	....	....		öffentlich
7	....	der Schatz	....	....
8	zerstören	....	....	....
9	....	....		aktuell
10	....	der Schutz	....	....

Strategy

'False friends'

'False friends' (also known as false cognates) are words which look or sound like English words but have a different meaning. There are relatively few of these in German.

B Was bedeuten folgende Wörter auf Englisch?

1 romanisch
2 römisch
3 der Fotograf
4 die Art
5 künstlich

6 bilden
7 der Alltag
8 die Plastik
9 das Motiv (*in art*)
10 mittelalterlich

6 Das Berliner Kulturleben damals und heute

der Alltag	everyday life
die Aufführung (-en)	performance
die Ausstellung (-en)	exhibition
die BRD / Bundesrepublik Deutschland	The FRG / Federal Republic of Germany
damalig	former
darstellen	to represent
die DDR / Deutsche Demokratische Republik	The GDR / German Democratic Republic
das Denkmal (¨e)	monument
die Einwohnerzahl	population
die Epoche (-n)	era
die Freiheit	freedom
früher (*adj*)	past (*adj*)
die Gedenkstätte (-n)	memorial
die Gegenwart	present day
gegenwärtig (*adj*)	present-day (*adj*)
die Grenze (-n)	border
gründen	to found
heutig	modern
der Krieg (-e)	war
das Kulturleben	cultural life
die Macht (¨e)	power
das Merkmal (-e)	feature, characteristic
mitten in der Stadt	right in the middle of the city
der Politiker (-)	politician
prägen	to characterise
die Regierung (-en)	government
der Staat (-en)	state, country
das Stadtbild	cityscape, skyline
stattfinden (i-a-u)	to take place
die Toleranz / tolerant	tolerance / tolerant
die Vergangenheit	the past
ein / das Volk (¨er)	a / the people
die Wiedervereinigung	reunification
das Zeitalter (-)	era, age

6.1 Berlin – geprägt durch seine Geschichte

Berlin – characterised by its history

abreißen (ei-i-i)	to demolish
angesehen (*adj*)	respected
das Ansehen	respect
aufblühen	to flourish
die Aufklärung	the Enlightenment
aufteilen	to divide
im Ausland	abroad
die Ausreiseerlaubnis	permission to leave
das Bauwerk (-e)	building
die Besatzungsarmee (-n)	army of occupation
die Besatzungszone (-n)	occupation zone
besetzen	to occupy
demonstrieren	to demonstrate
demontieren	to demolish, dismantle
der Denker (-)	thinker
der Dichter (-)	poet
ehemalig	former
das Elend	misery
(sich) entwickeln	to develop
das Ereignis (-se)	event, occurrence
errichten	to construct
die Errichtung	construction
die Freizügigkeit	freedom of movement
gesperrt	restricted
geteilt	divided
die Glaubensfreiheit	freedom of belief
die Grenzübergangsstelle (-n)	border checkpoint
der Kaiser (-)	emperor
der Kalte Krieg	the Cold War
die Nachkriegszeit	the post-war period
der Philosoph (-en)	philosopher
der Polizeispitzel (-)	police informer
das Regierungsviertel	area of government buildings
schlagartig	sudden(ly)
der Sektor (-en)	sector
sperren	to block, close
der Spion (-e)	spy
die Staatssicherheit / Stasi	DDR secret police

das Symbol (-e)	symbol
die Teilung Deutschlands	the division of Germany
der Umzug (⁻e)	move, relocation
vereinen	to unite
veröffentlichen	to publish
die Vorkriegszeit	the pre-war period
der Wachturm (⁻e)	watch-tower
die Währung (-en)	currency
wehrpflichtig	liable for military service
sich weigern	to refuse
der Weltkrieg (-e)	world war
die Wiedervereinigung	reunification
die Zone (-n)	zone

es wurde als (+*Nom*) ... anerkannt	it was recognised as…
er ließ (+*Acc*) ... bauen	he had…built
zu diesem Zeitpunkt	at that time
in den zwanziger Jahren	in the 1920s
das Land der Dichter und Denker	the land of poets and thinkers
die Berliner Luftbrücke	the Berlin Airlift (1948–49)
die Berliner Mauer	the Berlin Wall (1961–89)

Berlin im Dritten Reich	*Berlin in the Third Reich*
(sich) anpassen (+*Dat*)	to conform
der Antisemitismus	antisemitism
ausgrenzen	to exclude, marginalise
die Ausgrenzung	exclusion, marginalisation
ausrotten	to stamp out, eradicate
ausschließen (ie-o-o)	to exclude
der Austragungsort (-e)	venue (sport)
ausüben	to exercise, practise
bedrohen	to threaten
beschlagnahmen (*insep*)	to confiscate
der Boykott (-s)	boycott
boykottieren	to boycott
darstellen	to represent, portray
die Diktatur	dictatorship
drehen	to shoot (a film)
entartet	degenerate (*Nazi designation*)
entlassen (ä-ie-a)	to dismiss
die Entscheidung (-en)	decision

fernbleiben* (ei-ie-ie)	to stay away
fliehen* (ie-o-o)	to flee
die Flucht (-en)	escape
flüchten*	to flee
der Flüchtling (-e)	refugee
gelten (i-a-o) als	to be viewed as
die Gewaltherrschaft	tyranny
die Gleichschaltung	enforced conformity
der Häftling (-e)	prisoner, detainee
der Held (-en)	hero
hinrichten	to execute
der Jude (-n) / die Jüdin (-nen)	Jew
jüdisch	Jewish
die Kaserne (-n)	barracks
der Konzentrationslager (-)	concentration camp
die Kraft (¨e)	strength
die Kriegserklärung (-en)	declaration of war
die Machtergreifung	seizure of power
die Mannschaft (-en)	team
der Medaillenspiegel (-)	medals table
die Niederlage (-n)	defeat
die Olympiade	Olympic Games
das Opfer (-)	victim
der Regisseur (-e)	film director
der Schriftsteller (-)	author
sicherheitshalber	to be on the safe side
die Stärke (-n)	strength
teilnehmen (*irreg*) an (+*Dat*)	to take part in
unabhängig	independent
verbieten (ie-o-o)	to ban
verfolgen	to persecute
verhaften	to arrest
verpönen	to scorn
vertreiben (ei-ie-ie)	to expel
die Wehrmacht	the Army (*to 1945*)
zerstören	to destroy
zwingen (i-a-u)	to force

ihre Kunst wurde als ... angesehen	their art was regarded as…

6.2 Theater, Musik und Museen in Berlin

Theatre, music and museums in Berlin

abwechslungsreich	varied
alljährlich	annual
anziehen (*irreg*)	to attract
aufführen (*tr*)	to perform, stage
Aufsehen erregen	to cause a sensation
aufstrebend	aspiring
der Auftritt (-e)	appearance, performance
ausführlich	in detail
die Auswahl	selection
die Besetzung (-en)	cast (of play)
die Bühne (-n)	stage
das Bühnenbild (-er)	stage set
der Dirigent (-en)	conductor
dirigieren	to conduct
der Dramatiker (-)	dramatist
erleben	to experience
die Erstaufführung (-en)	premiere
gesellschaftskritisch	critical of society
großschreiben (ei-ie-ie)	to value
sich handeln um (+*Acc*)	to be about
die Handlung (-en)	plot (of drama etc.)
herrschen	to prevail, be predominant
die Inszenierung (-en)	production
der Klang (⁻e)	sound
der Konzertsaal (*pl* -säle)	concert hall
die Kulisse (-n)	scenery
der Kunstschatz (⁻e)	art treasure
die Leistung (-en)	achievement
mitreißend	thrilling
das Museum (*pl* Museen)	museum
der Mythos (*pl* Mythen)	myth
die Oper (-n)	opera / opera house
das Plakat (-e)	poster
der Regisseur (-)	director
die Sammlung (-en)	collection
der Schauspieler (-)	actor

das Sinfonieorchester (-)	symphony orchestra
der Spielplan (-̈e)	repertoire
das Theaterstück (-e)	play
unterhaltsam	entertaining
die Unterhaltung	entertainment
die Uraufführung (-en)	(world) premiere
die Veranstaltung (-en)	event (*pl* What's On)
verkörpern	to embody
der Vorhang (-̈e)	curtain
wechselvoll	varied
zahlreich	numerous
das Zeitalter (-)	epoch
zeitgenössisch	contemporary
die Zeitgeschichte	contemporary history
der Zuhörer (-)	listener (*pl* audience)
der Zuschauer (-)	spectator (*pl* audience)
der Zustand (-̈e)	condition

....

zum UNESCO-Welterbe gehören	to be a UNESCO World Heritage site
sich unterhalten lassen (ä-ie-a)	to be entertained
zur Verfügung stehen (*irreg*)	to be available, on offer
die einst geteilte Stadt Berlin	the once-divided city of Berlin
sie gehören zu den besten der Welt	they are among the best in the world

6.3 Die Vielfalt innerhalb der Bevölkerung Berlins
The diversity within the population of Berlin

abbauen	to break down
allmählich	gradual
die Altersgruppe (-n)	age group
der Anteil (-e)	share, amount
die Armut	poverty
der Ausländer (-)	foreigner
die Ausländerfeindlichkeit	xenophobia
austauschen	to exchange
behandeln	to treat, deal with
berufstätig	employed, in work
die Bevölkerung (-en)	population
der Bevölkerungsrückgang	decline in population
die Bevölkerungsschicht (-en)	population group

der Bevölkerungszuwachs	growth in population
die Beziehung (-en)	relationship
der Bezirk (-e)	district
dulden	to tolerate
einberufen (*tr*)	to call up, conscript
der Einheimische (*adj. noun*)	local person (resident)
die Einstellung (-en)	attitude
der Einwanderer (-)	immigrant
der Einwohner (-)	inhabitant
erwerbsfähig	able to work
fördern	to encourage, promote
der Gastarbeiter (-)	foreign worker (*1950s to 1970s*)
das Gemeindehaus (¨er)	community centre
die Gemeinschaft (-en)	community
die Gentrifizierung	gentrification
geteilt	divided
die Glaubensrichtung (-en)	religion, belief system
gleichgeschlechtlich	homosexual, same-sex
gleichgesinnt	like-minded
die Herkunft (¨e)	origin
hindeuten auf (+*Acc*)	to indicate
der Hintergrund (¨e)	background
der Kiez (-e)	neighbourhood
die Kinderbetreuung	childcare
die Kneipe (-n)	pub
locken	to attract, entice
das Mehrgenerationenhaus (¨er)	multigenerational house
die Miete (-n)	rent
die Minderheit (-en)	minority
die Moschee (-n)	mosque
multikulturell / multikulti (*inf*)	multicultural
das Nachtleben	night-life
die Nationalität (-en)	nationality
sich niederlassen (ä-ie-a)	to settle
sanieren	to renovate
schaffen (a-u-a)	to create
schwul	gay
die Sperrstunde (-n)	curfew, closing time
der Stadtteil (-e)	district
stammen aus (+*Dat*)	to originate from
der Treffpunkt (-¨e)	meeting place

der Überfall (⁼e)	attack; assault
überwiegend	predominantly
das Umfeld	environment, surroundings
unterstützen (*insep*)	to support
vermuten	to suspect
sich verständigen	to come to an understanding, communicate
das Vertrauen	trust
sich verwirklichen	to develop one's potential
vielfältig	diverse
die Vorfahren	ancestors
das Vorurteil (-e)	prejudice
Vorurteile abbauen	to overcome prejudices
sich wohlfühlen	to feel at ease
der Wohnstandort (-e)	suburban district
zahlreich	numerous
der Zufluchtsort (-e)	place of refuge
der Zuzug (⁼e)	influx

---

aus allen Bevölkerungsschichten	from all walks of life
sie sind ausländischer Herkunft	they are of foreign origin
sie sind deutscher Abstammung	they have German roots
mit Migrationshintergrund	(s.o.) from a migrant background
jeder sechste Berliner ist Ausländer	one in six Berliners is a foreigner
das rasante Wachstum	rapid growth
sich durch Aushilfsjobs über Wasser halten (ä-ie-a)	to keep one's head above water by doing temporary jobs

Websites

You will find other useful articles, links and vocabulary on this topic on the following websites:

www.in-berlin-brandenburg.com

www.berlin.de

Strategy

Compound nouns: noun + noun formation

As well as constructions such as adjective + noun (p. 53), compound nouns can be formed from two nouns; the first noun may be in its plural form, or in the genitive **-(e)s-**. Even some feminine nouns add **-(e)s-**! But many nouns are used just in their singular form; look carefully at how compound nouns consisting of noun + noun are formed when you encounter them.

A Wie werden die folgenden zusammengesetzten Substantive verbunden? Notieren Sie für das erste Substantiv in jedem Wort: **Plural** (-(e)n-, -e-, -er-), **Genitiv** (-(e)s-), oder **einfaches Substantiv** (Subst.).
1 die Bundesrepublik
2 die Einwohnerzahl
3 das Stadtbild
4 das Regierungsviertel
5 der Polizeispitzel
6 der Weltkrieg
7 das Bühnenbild
8 der Konzertsaal
9 die Altersgruppe
10 der Kindergarten

Strategy

Weak masculine nouns

Most masculine nouns which add **-(e)n** in the plural are weak nouns; in fact, they add **-(e)n** in *all* forms except the nominative singular. Almost all of them refer to male persons or animals. (There is no real reason for the designation 'weak'.)

B Welche der folgenden Substantive sind *keine* schwachen Nomen? Notieren Sie auch die englische Bedeutung jedes Substantivs.
1 der Philosoph
2 der Einwohner
3 der Jude
4 der Dirigent
5 der Polizist
6 der Automat
7 der Architekt
8 der Flüchtling
9 der Mensch
10 der Held

Section B   Film and literature

B1 Film   *Film*

die Besetzung (-en)	cast
der Filmstar (-s)	film star
ein Film über (+Acc)	a film about
freigegeben ab 12 Jahren	Certificate 12 (film rating)
das Genre (-s)	genre
die Handlung (-en)	plot, action
die Komödie (-n)	comedy
eine Rolle spielen	to play a part
der Schauplatz (⸚e)	scene (where film takes place)
der Schauspieler (-)	actor
der Spielfilm (-e)	feature film
die Szene (-n)	scene (in film)
der Ton	soundtrack
die Vorstellung (-en)	showing (of film)
der Zeichentrickfilm (-e)	cartoon

aktionsreich	action-packed
die Atmosphäre	atmosphere
der Auszug (⸚e)	extract
die Beleuchtung	lighting
beschleunigen / die Beschleunigung	to accelerate / acceleration
die Computeranimation	animatronics
der Dialog (-e)	dialogue
das Drehbuch (⸚er)	screenplay
durchfallen* (ä-ie-a)	to flop
der Erfolg (-e)	success
das Filmset (-s)	set
der Flop (-s)	flop
die Folge (-n) / das Sequel (-s)	sequel
die Froschperspektive	worm's-eye view
der Hauptdarsteller (-)	leading actor
die Hauptrolle (-n)	leading part
der Kinobesucher (-)	cinema-goer

der Kinorenner (-)	box-office hit
der Klassiker (-)	classic
der Knüller (-)	blockbuster
die Leinwand / die Bildwand	(cinema) screen
die Naheinstellung (-en)	close-up
die Originalfassung (-en)	original version
Regie führen bei (+*Dat*)	to direct
der Regisseur (-e)	director
die Rückblende (-n)	flash-back
der Schwenk (-s)	panning shot
die Spezialeffekte	special effects
synchronisieren	to dub
englisch synchronisiert	dubbed into English
der Trailer (-) / die Vorschau	trailer
die Vogelperspektive	bird's-eye view
das Voiceover	voice-over
der Zeitsprung (⁻e)	jump in time
die Zuschauer (*pl*) / das Publikum	audience
ein Zeitsprung in die Vergangenheit / Zukunft	a jump backwards / forwards in time
der Film ist nun überall zu sehen	the film is on general release
eine Oscar-Nominierung erhalten (ä-ie-a)	to receive an Oscar nomination
eine packende Thematik	exciting subject matter
freigegeben ab 16 Jahren	an adult film
einen Film drehen	to make a film
mit deutschen Untertiteln	with German subtitles
die Kamera schwenkte auf die Gruppe ein	the camera panned into the group

B2 Literatur *Literature*

beschreiben (ei-ie-ie)	to describe
ein Buch über (+*Acc*)	a book about
darstellen	to portray
erzählen / die Erzählung (-en)	to recount, tell / short story
die Fantasie	imagination
handeln von (+*Dat*) / die Handlung (-en)	to be about / plot
das Kapitel (-)	chapter
der Leser (-)	reader

der Reißer (-) / der Thriller (-)	thriller
der Roman (-e)	novel
das Sachbuch (¨er)	non-fiction
der Schriftsteller (-)	writer, author

der Absatz (¨e)	paragraph
der Ausgang	ending, dénouement
der Ausschnitt (-e)	extract
die Bedeutung (-en)	meaning
die Belletristik	fiction and poetry
der Bildungsroman (-e)	novel about the development of a character
der Bücherwurm (¨er)	book worm
der Charakter	character (personality)
die Charakterisierung	characterisation
darstellen / schildern	to portray
der Dialog (-e)	dialogue
der Dichter (-)	poet
die Dichtung	literature, poetry
das Drama	drama
entfalten (*tr*) / sich entfalten (*itr*)	to unfold
entwickeln (*tr*) / sich entwickeln (*itr*)	to develop
erfunden	imaginary
der Erzähler (-)	narrator
die Gattung (-en)	genre
das Gedicht (-e)	poem
die Gestalt (-en) / die Figur (-en)	character (person, figure)
die Gruselgeschichte (-n)	horror story
das Happy End	happy end
die Hauptfigur (-en)	main character
der Held (-en)	hero
die Idee (-n)	idea
die Jugendliteratur	literature for young people
der Klappentext	blurb
die Leseratte (-n)	book worm
der Liebesroman (-e)	romantic novel
das Meisterwerk (-e)	masterpiece
die Nebenhandlung (-en)	sub-plot
die Novelle (-n)	novella
die Poesie	poetry
die Prosa	prose

quasi autobiografisch	semi-autobiographical
die Sammlung (-en)	collection
schließlich	in the end
das Taschenbuch (-̈er)	paperback
übersetzen (insep)	to translate
verarbeiten	to deal with (subject)
verbinden (i-a-u) / die Verbindung (-en)	to link / link
das Verhältnis (-se)	relationship
veröffentlichen	to publish
der Vorgang (-̈e)	event
das Werk (-e) / gesammelte Werke	work / complete works
die Zeile (-n)	line

....

es dreht sich um (+Acc)	it concerns, is about…
es setzt sich kritisch mit (+Dat) … auseinander	it takes a critical look at…
eine Erzählung in der Ich- / Er-Form	a story in the first / third person
der allwissende Erzähler	the omniscient narrator
es spielt in (+Dat)	it is set in…
der Schauplatz der Erzählung	the scene of the story
im Laufe der Geschichte	in the course of the story
im Mittelpunkt des Romans	at the heart of the novel
menschliche Beziehungen	human relationships
sein Verhältnis zu seiner Frau	his relationship with his wife
sich (Dat) etw. vorstellen	to imagine sth.
sich mit einer Figur identifizieren	to identify with a character
ein starkes gesellschaftliches Engagement	a strong social conscience
eine moralisch fundierte Sozialkritik	social criticism with a moral basis
die Schattenseiten (pl) des Wirtschaftswunders	the downside to the economic miracle
es artikuliert sich in (+Dat)	it is expressed in…
zum Thema werden* (i-u-o)	to become an issue
die Nöte und Sorgen der kleinen Leute	the problems and worries of ordinary people
das menschliche Scheitern	human failure
ich konnte das Buch einfach nicht aus der Hand legen	I just couldn't put the book down

B3 Ein Buch / einen Film beschreiben

Describing a book / film

der Aufbau	form, structure
behandeln / die Behandlung	to deal with / treatment
beschreiben (ei-ie-ie)	to describe
die Eigenschaft (-en)	characteristic
enttäuschend	disappointing
entwickeln (*tr*) / die Entwicklung (-en)	to develop / development
das Ereignis (-se)	event
erklären	to explain
ernsthaft	serious
der Humor	(sense of) humour
humorvoll / heiter	humorous
interpretieren / die Interpretation	to interpret / interpretation
lebendig	lively, vivid
die Perspektive (-n)	perspective
schaffen (a-u-a)	to create
schildern	to portray
spannend	exciting
die Spannung (-en)	tension, excitement
die Sprache (-n) / sprachlich	language / linguistic
der Stil (-e)	style
das Thema (*pl* Themen)	subject
unterhaltsam	entertaining
unverständlich	incomprehensible
jdm. zusagen	to appeal to s.o.

die Absicht (-en)	intention
analysieren / die Analyse	to analyse / analysis
ausdrücken	to express
berühren	to touch on
der Bezugspunkt (-e)	point of reference
die Erzähltechnik	narrative technique
der Handlungswechsel (-)	twist in the plot
der Höhepunkt (-e)	climax
der Kommentar (-e)	commentary
die Kritik (-en)	critique, criticism
kritisieren	to criticise
kultiviert	cultured (person)

die Lehre (-n)	moral point
das Motiv (-e)	motive, motif (= image)
auf etw. (+Acc) reagieren	to react to sth.
schätzen	to appreciate (art, music)
das Symbol (-e)	symbol
die Symbolik	symbolism
thematisch	as regards subject matter
etw. thematisieren	to take sth. as a central theme
das Unbehagen an (+Dat)	unease, disquiet at…
vergleichen (ei-i-i)	to compare
verkörpern	to personify
vermitteln	to convey
wirken als	to act as
die Wortwahl	choice of words
zitieren / das Zitat (-e)	to quote / quotation
die Zusammenfassung (-en)	summary

etw. in Frage stellen	to question sth.
die Hauptthemen hervorheben (e-o-o)	to emphasise the main themes
Was können wir daraus entnehmen?	What can we draw / infer from this?
es lässt an (+Acc) … denken	it suggests, evokes…
eine Reflexion über (+Acc)	a reflection on…
eine kritische Einstellung zu (+Dat)	a critical attitude to…
ein zentrales Thema	a central theme
der erzählerische Stil	narrative style
es fand bei den Kritikern wenig Lob	it met with little praise from the critics
der gesellschaftliche / historische Hintergrund	the social / historical background

Positives	Positive points
beachtlich	relevant, excellent
die Einfühlung in (+Acc)	empathy with
ergreifend / rührend	moving
fesselnd	gripping
gefühlstief	intense
gefühlvoll	sensitive
genial	inspired
glanzvoll	sparkling
glaubwürdig	believable
ideenreich / der Ideenreichtum	imaginative / inventiveness
lebensnah	true to life

Film and literature

leicht verständlich	easily understood
(sehr) lesenswert	(well) worth reading
liebevoll	affectionate
optimistisch	optimistic
stimmungsvoll	full of atmosphere
überzeugend	convincing
unterhaltsam / kurzweilig	entertaining
warmherzig	warm-hearted
wirkungsvoll	effective
witzig	witty
zeitlos	timeless
zutreffend	accurate

wir fühlen uns in seine Lage hineinversetzt	we imagine ourselves in his position
einer der bedeutendsten Romane	one of the most significant novels
konsequent durchdacht	well thought-out

Negatives — *Negative points*

banal	banal
belanglos / trivial	trivial
dürftig	insubstantial
das Klischee (-s)	cliché
voller Klischees	full of clichés
klischeehaft	stereotyped
mittelmäßig	mediocre
monoton	repetitive
plump	crude, obvious
schwer zu lesen	unreadable
schwerfällig	clumsy
simpel	simplistic
sinnlos	meaningless
trist	drab
trocken	dry, uninspired
unglaubwürdig	unbelievable
unlogisch	illogical
unwahrscheinlich	improbable, unlikely
vage	vague
verwickelt / kompliziert	involved, convoluted
weit ausholend / weitschweifig	long-winded
zusammenhanglos	disjointed

Neutrales	*Neutral points*
anspruchslos	undemanding, lowbrow
anspruchsvoll	demanding, highbrow
aufwühlend	disturbing
ausführlich	detailed
bildlich	figuratively
brutal	violent
buchstäblich / wortwörtlich	literally
didaktisch	didactic, with a message
idealistisch	idealistic
ironisch	ironic
kompromisslos	uncompromising
kühl, distanziert	detached, impersonal
nostalgisch	nostalgic
pessimistisch	pessimistic
präzise	precise
realistisch	realistic
rührselig / sentimental	sentimental
sachlich	unemotional
schlicht / die Schlichtheit	simple / simplicity
skurril	droll, comical
umstritten	controversial
verzweifelt	despairing
zusammenschließen (ie-o-o)	to combine, bring together

es stellt hohe Ansprüche an den Leser	it makes great demands on the reader
es lässt den Leser selbst Schlüsse ziehen	it lets the reader draw his/her own conclusions
wir bekommen dadurch einen Einblick in (+Acc)	it gives us an insight into…

7 Einwanderung

die Angst (¨e)	fear
die Anzahl	number (approximate)
die Arbeitskraft (¨e)	worker
der Arbeitsplatz (¨e)	job
die Armut	poverty
der Asylant (-en)	asylum-seeker
die Ausländerfeindlichkeit	xenophobia
auswandern* / die Auswanderung	to emigrate / emigration
die Bevölkerung (-en)	population
der Bildungsstand (¨e)	level of education
der Bürger (-)	citizen
der Bürgerkrieg (-e)	civil war
jdn. diskriminieren	to discriminate against s.o.
die Diskriminierung	discrimination
der Einheimische (*adj. noun*)	local (person), native
die Einstellung (-en)	attitude
der Einwanderer (-)	immigrant
die Einwanderung / die Zuwanderung	immigration
der Einwohner (-)	inhabitant
das Entwicklungsland (¨er)	developing country
fliehen* vor (+*Dat*) (ie-o-o)	to flee from
der Flüchtling (-e)	refugee
der Fremde (*adj. noun*)	foreigner, stranger
die Fremdenfeindlichkeit	xenophobia
die Gesellschaft (-en)	society
die Großstadt (¨e)	city
das Herkunftsland (¨er)	country of origin
hoch qualifiziert	highly qualified
der Krieg (-e)	war
das Kriegsgebiet (-e)	war zone
die Krise (-n)	crisis
lösen	to solve

der Rassismus	racism
die Spannung (-en)	tension
ungelernt	unskilled
die Ursache (-n)	cause
der Zuzug (-̈e)	influx

7.1 Die Gründe für Migration   *The reasons for migration*

das Abkommen (-)	agreement
der Andersgläubige (*adj. noun*)	s.o. of a different faith
als … anerkannt werden* (i-u-o)	to be recognised as…
die Angehörigen	relatives
einen Asylantrag stellen	to apply for asylum
der Asylbewerber (-)	asylum applicant
das Ausmaß	extent
der Aussiedler (-)	ethnic German immigrant
benachteiligt	disadvantaged
bestehen (*irreg*) aus (+*Dat*)	to exist / to consist of
die Bevölkerung	population
der Bildungsabschluss (-̈e)	qualification
dauerhaft	permanent
der Dschihad	jihad
ehemalig	former
ehrgeizig	ambitious
das Elend	misery
fehlend	inadequate
die Flüchtlingskrise (-n)	refugee crisis
die Flut (-en)	flood
die Geburtenrate (-n)	birth-rate
sich gewöhnen an (+*Acc*)	to get used to
die Globalisierung	globalisation
die Grundkenntnisse (*pl*)	basic knowledge
die Heimat	homeland
das Heimweh	homesickness
die Hoffnung (-en)	hope
illegal	illegal
die Intoleranz	intolerance
die Klimaerwärmung	global warming
der Klimawandel	climate change
der Konflikt (-e)	conflict

die Korruption	corruption
die Krise (-n)	crisis
die Lage (-n)	situation
die Lebensbedingungen	living conditions
leiden (*irreg*) unter (+*Dat*)	to suffer from
die Menschenrechte	human rights
die Menschenrechtsverletzung (-en)	abuse of human rights
der Mittelmeerstaat (-en)	Mediterranean country
das Motiv (-e)	motive
das Nachbarland (-̈er)	neighbouring country
(jdn.) nachholen	to bring (s.o.) to join one
die Naturkatastrophe (-n)	natural disaster
die Perspektive (-n)	prospects
die Polizeibrutalität	police brutality
die Schlepperbande (-n)	(people-)smuggling ring
schützen	to protect
die Staatsangehörigkeit	nationality
der Staatsbürger (-)	citizen
die Staatsbürgerschaft	citizenship
stammen aus (+*Dat*)	to come from
steigen* (ei-ie-ie)	to rise, increase
der Totalitarismus / totalitär	totalitarianism / totalitarian
überschreiten (ei-i-i) (*insep*)	to exceed
die Umweltzerstörung	environmental destruction
unzureichend	inadequate
verbessern	to improve
verfolgen / die Verfolgung	to persecute / persecution
vergeblich	in vain
die Verhältnisse	circumstances
sich verschlechtern	to get worse
das Wachstum	growth
der Wirtschaftsflüchtling (-e)	economic migrant
wohlhabend	wealthy
das Ziel (-e)	goal, destination

....

auf der Suche nach einem besseren Leben	in the search for a better life
fehlende Bildungschancen	poor educational opportunities
die Schätzungen gehen weit auseinander	estimates vary greatly
die Statistik belegt, dass ...	statistics show that...

die Hoffnung auf ein besseres Leben	the hope for a better life
sie haben keine andere Wahl	they have no other choice
der islamische Fundamentalismus	Islamic fundamentalism

Migration in der Nachkriegszeit — *Post-war migration*

abschließen (ie-o-o)	to complete, negotiate
der Anwerbestopp	ban on recruitment
die Arbeitserlaubnis (-se)	work permit
der Aufenthalt	stay, period of residence
die Baustelle (-n)	building site
befristet	temporary
der Bergbau	coal-mining industry
bezeichnen als	to characterise as
die Einrichtung (-en)	institution
das Etagenbett (-en)	bunk beds
die Fähigkeit (-en)	skill
der Fahrzeugbau	vehicle manufacturing
der Familienangehörige (*adj. noun*)	family member
das Fließband (¨er)	conveyor belt, assembly line
am Fließband arbeiten	to work on a production line
das Gastgewerbe	hotel and restaurant industry
gefragt	in demand
die Gemeinschaftsunterkunft (¨e)	shared accommodation
knapp (*adj*)	scarce
der Kohlebergbau	coal mining
die Landwirtschaft	agriculture
die Schichtarbeit	shift work
das Schienennetz (-e)	rail network
die Schwerindustrie	heavy industry
in den sechziger Jahren	in the 1960s
der Straßenbau	road construction
die Tätigkeit (-en)	activity
ungelernte Arbeitskräfte	unskilled workers
verlängern	to extend
verteilen	to spread
der Wiederaufbau	reconstruction
wiederbeleben (*tr*)	to revitalise
die Wirtschaftslage	state of the economy
das Wirtschaftswunder	economic miracle
wohlhabend	prosperous
die Wohnbedingung (-en)	living conditions

das Wohnheim (-e)	hostel
zerstört	destroyed
zunehmend	increasing
zurückkehren*	to return
der Zusammenhang (-̈e)	connection

7.2 Vor- und Nachteile der Einwanderung
Advantages and disadvantages of immigration

(gut) abschneiden (*irreg*)	to do well (in test)
anerkennen (e-a-a)	to recognise
sich anfreunden	to become friends
der Arbeitskräftebedarf	the need for workers
aufgrund (+*Gen*)	on the basis of
ausbeuten ⎫ ausnutzen ⎭	to exploit
ausgeschlossen	isolated
ausgrenzen / die Ausgrenzung	to exclude / exclusion
befürworten	to support
beherrschen	to master
die Berufsausbildung	job training
die Beschränkung (-en)	limit
betteln	to beg
sich bewerben (i-a-o) um (+*Acc*)	to apply for
die Branche (-n)	(area of) industry, business
eintreffen* (i-a-o)	to arrive
erwerben (i-a-o)	to acquire
das Erwerbseinkommen	income from employment
erwerbstätig	employed
die Fachkraft (-̈e)	qualified worker
der Fachkräftemangel	shortage of qualified personnel
der Fremde (*adj. noun*)	stranger
der Geburtenrückgang	declining birth-rate
die Gefahr (-en)	danger
gefährden	to endanger
gering	small
gewohnt	accustomed
der Haushalt	budget
herstellen	to produce, manufacture
hochwertig (*adj*)	high-quality, high-grade

die Konkurrenzfähigkeit ⎫ die Wettbewerbsfähigkeit ⎭	competitiveness
mangeln	to lack
die Masseneinwanderung	mass immigration
die Miete (-n)	rent
der Missbrauch	abuse, assault
die Personalbeschaffung	recruitment
die Pflege	care
das Rentenalter	retirement age
selbstbewusst	self-confident
die Sicherheit	security
studieren	to study
temporär	temporary
der Terrorist (-en)	terrorist
die Überalterung	disproportionate number of old people
überfordert werden* (i-u-o)	to be overstretched
die Überschwemmung	swamping
das Unternehmen (-)	firm, business
der Verlust (-e)	loss
die Verständigung	understanding
die Wanderungsbilanz ⎫ der Wanderungssaldo ⎭	net migration
das Wohlbefinden	welfare

- - -

einen Beitrag leisten	to make a contribution
die Kultur des Landes bereichern	to enrich the culture of the country
eine Gemeinde unter Druck setzen	to put a community under pressure
den Bedarf an Fachkräften (*pl*) decken	to meet the demand for skilled personnel
die Wirtschaft ist auf Fachkräfte aus dem Ausland angewiesen	the economy is reliant on skilled workers from abroad
von sozialen Leistungen (*pl*) leben	to live off social security
die rapide Alterung der Gesellschaft	a society that is aging rapidly
soziale Spannungen	social tensions
der Westen hat den Glauben an sich verloren	The West has lost its faith in itself
eine Person mit Migrationshintergrund	s.o. whose parents are not German
der demografische Wandel	demographic change

Wirtschaftliche Aspekte — *Economic aspects*

anstellen / einstellen	to employ
die Anwerbung (-en)	recruitment
der Arbeitgeber (-)	employer
der Arbeitnehmer (-)	employee
die Arbeitsgenehmigung (-en)	work permit
der Arbeitsvertrag (¨e)	employment contract
die Ausbildung	training
das Bedürfnis (-se)	need
der Beitrag (¨e)	contribution
die Beschäftigung (-en)	employment
der Betrieb (-e)	business, company
bevorzugen	to prefer
das Bildungsniveau	level of education
die Deutschkenntnisse (*pl*)	knowledge of German
das Einkommen (-)	income
erwerben (i-a-o)	to acquire
die Fähigkeit (-en)	skill, ability
gefragt	in demand
die Gesundheitsfürsorge	health care
herstellen	to produce, manufacture
der Hochschulabschluss (¨e)	(university) degree
der Mindestlohn (¨e)	minimum wage
der Sprachkurs (-e)	language course
die Umschulung	retraining
die Unterkunft (¨e)	accommodation, lodging
unterstützen (*insep*)	to support, help
der Wirtschaftswissenschaftler (-)	economist
der Zugang (¨e)	access

Politische Aspekte — *Political aspects*

abschieben (ie-o-o)	to deport
anpacken	to tackle
der Anspruch (¨e)	right, claim
die Anstrengung (-en)	effort
die Aufenthaltserlaubnis (-se)	residence permit
aufrechterhalten (ä-ie-a)	to maintain
belasten / die Belastung (-en)	to burden / burden, load
berücksichtigen	to take into consideration

beschleunigen	to speed up
die Einbürgerung	naturalisation
eindämmen	to control, reduce
sich einsetzen für (+Acc)	to stand up for
die Entlastung	relief (of burden, strain)
fördern	to support, encourage
die Freizügigkeit	freedom of movement
gerecht	just, fair
gewähren	to provide, allow
heimisch	native
die Herausforderung (-en)	challenge
hiesig	local
integrieren	to integrate
der Konsens	consensus
konsequent	consistent, logical
die Krankenversicherung (-en)	health insurance
das Kriterium (pl Kriterien)	criterion (pl criteria)
künftig (adj)	future (adj)
der Mitgliedsstaat (-en)	member state
die Nettozuwanderung	net migration
die Prognose (-n)	forecast
die Quote (-n)	quota
das Recht (-e) auf (+Acc)	right, entitlement to
die Regierung (-en)	government
die Schätzung (-en)	estimate
schrumpfen* (itr)	to shrink, dwindle
schutzbedürftig	needing protection
die Steuerung (-en)	management, control
umgehend	immediate, prompt
die Vereinbarung (-en)	agreement
das Verfahren (-)	process
das Verhältnis (-se)	relationship
verhandeln	to negotiate
das Versagen	failure
völkerrechtlich	under international law
vorlegen	to present
Vorsorge (pl) treffen (i-a-o)	to make provision, take precautions
der Wert (-e)	worth, (moral) value
die Zahl begrenzen	to limit numbers
zugelassen (adj)	approved, permitted

Einspruch erheben (e-o-o) gegen	to appeal against
den Missbrauch bekämpfen	to fight abuse
europäische Werte	European values
in den sauren Apfel beißen	to grasp the nettle
die Hürden für Hochqualifizierte senken	to reduce the hurdles for highly qualified people
die Einwanderungsbeschränkungen lockern	to relax immigration quotas
das Recht, seine Grenzen zu kontrollieren	the right to control one's borders
finanzielle Anreize zur Rückkehr in die Heimat	financial inducements to return home

---

Websites

You will find other useful articles, links and vocabulary on this topic on the following websites:

www.bamf.de *Federal office for Migration and Refugees*

www.bpb.de/gesellschaft/migration

Strategy

Forming adjectives and adverbs

Quite apart from words which exist as adjectives in their own right, it is possible to form adjectives by using the present or past participle, or adding a suffix such as **-bar**, **-haft**, **-ig**, **-isch**, **-lich** (with ¨ if possible), **-los**, **-voll** or **-sam** to a verb stem or noun. (Remember that adjectives and adverbs are normally grammatically identical.)

A Bilden Sie aus den folgenden Substantiven und Verben Adjektive. Notieren Sie sie mit ihren englischen Bedeutungen.
1 die Angst
2 diskriminieren
3 benachteiligen
4 der Ehrgeiz
5 abschließen
6 das Ausland
7 das Wunder
8 ausbilden
9 die Hoffnung
10 der Wert

Strategy

Verbs + prepositions

Many verbs are used with particular prepositions, some of which may not be the ones English-speakers would expect – and occasionally, there may be no preposition at all, where English-speakers would expect one. When you encounter them, note these combinations, along with the case taken by the preposition.

B Welche Präposition mit welchem Kasus verwendet man mit jedem Verb? Welches Verb braucht keine Präposition vor dem direkten Objekt?
1 bestehen .... (*to consist of*)
2 sich gewöhnen .... (*to get used to*)
3 mangeln .... (*to lack, be short of*)
4 leiden .... (*to suffer from*)
5 stammen .... (*to come from*)
6 sich bewerben .... (*to apply for*)
7 diskriminieren .... (*to discriminate against*)
8 schützen .... (*to protect from*)
9 suchen .... (*to look for*)
10 hoffen .... (*to hope for*)

8 Integration

angehen (*irreg*) / … geht alle an	to concern / …concerns everybody
aufnehmen (*irreg*)	to take in, include
behindern	to hinder, obstruct
die Bildung	education
die Chancengleichheit	equality of opportunity
die Demokratie (-n)	democracy
die Erfahrung (-en)	experience
der Erfolg (-e) / erfolgreich	success / successful
die ethnische Minderheit (-en)	ethnic minority
die Freiheit	freedom
helfen (i-a-o) / die Hilfe	to help / help
die Herausforderung (-en)	challenge
die Herkunft (¨e)	origin
das Hindernis (-se)	obstacle
die Integration	integration
die Kultur (-en)	culture
die Lebensweise (-n)	way of life
die Maßnahme (-n)	measure
misstrauen (+*Dat*) / das Misstrauen	to mistrust / mistrust
(Person) mit Migrationshintergrund	immigrant / s.o. born to non-German parents
die multikulturelle Gesellschaft	multicultural society
die Politik	politics / policy
Rechte und Pflichten	rights and responsibilities
die Rechtsstaatlichkeit	the rule of law
schützen vor (+*Dat*)	to protect from
der Sozialstaat (-en)	welfare state
stammen aus (+*Dat*)	to come from
tolerant / die Toleranz	tolerant / tolerance
unterstützen (*insep*)	to support
sich verbessern	to improve, get better
verstehen (*irreg*)	to understand
das Vorurteil (-e)	prejudice
weltoffen	cosmopolitan, liberal(-minded)
wettbewerbsfähig ⎫ konkurrenzfähig ⎭	competitive
wirksam	effective
der Zuzug (¨e)	influx

8.1 Maßnahmen zur Integration

Offizielle Maßnahmen	*Official measures*
abschaffen	to abolish
die Arbeitserlaubnis (-se)	work permit
der Arbeitsmarkt	the job market
die Ausländerbehörde (-n)	immigration authority
die Behörden	authorities
beraten (ä-ie-a) / die Beratung	to advise / advice
das Berufsleben	working life
bundesweit	across the whole of Germany
entwickeln (*tr*) / sich entwickeln (*itr*)	to develop
erleichtern	to make easier
erwarten / die Erwartung (-en)	to expect, expectation
erziehen (*irreg*)	to educate
die Fähigkeit (-en)	skill
fordern	to expect, require
fördern	to encourage, promote
Fortschritte (*pl*) machen	to make progress
die Gesellschaft (-en)	society
koordinieren	to co-ordinate
die Landesregierung (-en)	government of a federal state
landesweit	across a *Bundesland*
ins Leben rufen (u-ie-u)	to start up
das Musterbeispiel (-e)	prime example
die Nationalhymne (-n)	national anthem
die Notunterkunft (¨e)	emergency accommodation
die Obdachlosigkeit	homelessness
der Orientierungskurs (-e)	orientation course
die Pflicht (-en)	duty
die positive Diskriminierung	positive discrimination
das Prinzip (-ien)	principle
das Projekt (-e)	project
die Religionsfreiheit	freedom of religion
die Staatsbürgerschaft	citizenship
jdn. zu(r) Toleranz erziehen (*irreg*)	to teach s.o. to be tolerant
umfassen (*insep*) / umfassend (*adj*)	to include, contain / comprehensive
verpflichtet sein* (*irreg*)	to be obliged
die Werte	(moral, cultural) values

die Wirtschaft	economy
wirtschaftlich	economic, economically
das Zuwanderungsgesetz	immigration legislation

Gesellschaftliche Maßnahmen — *Measures taken in society*

das Alltagsleben	everyday life
ausgrenzen / die Ausgrenzung	to exclude / exclusion
begegnen* (+Dat)	to meet, encounter
die Begegnung (-en)	meeting
berücksichtigen	to take into consideration
die Debatte (-n)	debate
der Ehrenamtliche (*adj. noun*)	voluntary helper
einbeziehen (*irreg*)	to include
die Einbeziehung	inclusion
die Eingliederung	integration
empfangen (ä-i-a)	to receive / welcome
sich engagieren für (+Acc)	to be committed to
engagiert	committed
freiwillig	voluntary, voluntarily
ein Gespräch führen	to hold a conversation
motiviert	motivated
sich die Mühe machen	to take the trouble
der Neuankömmling (-e)	new arrival
das Selbstvertrauen	self-confidence
teilnehmen (*irreg*) an (+Dat)	to take part in
das Unternehmen (-)	business, company
der Unternehmer (-)	employer
das Verfahren (-)	process
sich vertraut machen mit (+Dat)	to familiarise o.s. with
das Vorbild (-er)	role model
jdn. willkommen heißen (ei-ie-ei)	to welcome s.o.
sich wohlfühlen	to feel at home
das Wohngebiet (-e)	residential area
sich zurechtfinden (i-a-u) in (+Dat)	to find one's way
zurechtkommen* (o-a-o)	to cope

Maßnahmen treffen (i-a-o), ergreifen (ei-i-i)	to take steps to do sth.
soziale Leistungen	welfare benefits
aus unterschiedlichen Kulturen	from different cultures
auf nationaler / lokaler Ebene	at national / local level

das Problem langfristig lösen	to find a long-term solution to the problem
Migranten mit … vertraut machen	to familiarise immigrants with…
Integration erfordert gegenseitigen Respekt / Achtung	integration requires mutual respect
unsere Art zu leben achten	to respect how we live
sich auf Deutsch verständigen können	to be able to make o.s. understood in German

8.2 Hindernisse für die Integration

Obstacles to integration

Probleme für das Gastland	***Problems for the host country***
abschrecken / die Abschreckung	to deter / deterrence
sich mit jdm. anfreunden	to make friends with s.o.
Angst haben (*irreg*) vor (+*Dat*)	to be frightened of
ausländisch	foreign
das Aussehen	appearance
der Außenseiter (-)	outsider
der Brauch (⁻e)	custom
einheimisch	local
der Einheimische (*adj. noun*)	local (person), native
fremd	foreign, alien, strange
das Getto (-s)	ghetto
zum Hindernis werden* (i-u-o)	to become an obstacle
das Kopftuch (⁻er), der Hidschab	headscarf, hijab
die Minderheit (-en)	minority
die Sicherheit	security, safety
die Überfremdung	swamping with foreigners
unterbringen (*irreg*)	to accommodate
das Verständnis	understanding
die Weltanschauung (-en)	world view, weltanschauung
ein Zeichen setzen	to set an example

Die Probleme der Einwanderer	***The problems of immigrants***
sich abkapseln	to cut / shut o.s. off
analphabetisch / der Analphabet	illiterate
arbeitslos / die Arbeitslosigkeit	unemployed / unemployment
aufgeben (i-a-e)	to give up
die Ausbildung	training

beantragen bei (+*Dat*)	to apply to…for sth.
benachteiligen	to put at a disadvantage / discriminate against
bereit	willing, ready
bestreiten (ei-i-i)	to dispute, deny
der Betroffene (*adj. noun*)	person affected
der Bildungsabschluss (¨e)	educational qualifications
bildungsfern / ungebildet	uneducated
das Bildungsniveau	level of education
brauchen	to need
die Denkweise (-n)	mind-set, way of thinking
die Deutschkenntnisse (*pl*)	knowledge of German
erschweren	to make more difficult
erwerbslos	unemployed
das Gesetz (-e)	law
die Gewalt	violence
die häusliche Gewalt	domestic violence
die Glaubensfreiheit	freedom of worship, religion
die Gleichheit der Geschlechter	equality of the sexes
grundverschieden	fundamentally different
die Hilfe	help
die Ignoranz	ignorance
niedrig	low
pflegebedürftig	in need of care
der Rassismus / rassistisch	racism / racist
scheitern* an (+*Dat*)	to fail (because of…)
das Schlusslicht bilden	to bring up the rear
sich mit (+*Dat*) schwertun (u-a-a)	to have problems with
die Sitte (-n)	custom
Steuern zahlen	to pay taxes
die Übergangsphase (-n)	transition phase
überwinden (i-a-u) (*insep*)	to overcome
unbegreiflich	inconceivable
die Unterkunft (¨e)	accommodation
vermeiden (ei-ie-ie)	to avoid
die Wurzel (-n)	root
die Zufluchtsstätte (-n)	house of refuge
sich zugehörig fühlen	to have a sense of belonging
die Zugehörigkeit	sense of belonging
der Zwang (¨e)	force, obligation

die Zwangsverheiratung (-en)	forced marriage
zwingen (i-a-u)	to force, oblige

sie werden durch (+Acc) ... benachteiligt	they are at a disadvantage because of…
kulturelle Unterschiede	cultural differences
keine Bleibe haben (irreg)	to have nowhere to stay
die Zahl der ... wird auf (eine Million) geschätzt	the number of…is estimated at (a million)
die Sprache beherrschen	to master the language
sie wollen in die Heimat zurück	they want to return home
sie haben keinen Kontakt zu ...	they have no contact with…
der Einstieg in den Arbeitsmarkt	getting into the job market
er passt nicht wirklich in ...	he doesn't really fit into…
manche finden es schwierig, in der deutschen Gesellschaft anzukommen	some find it hard to get on with German society
Deutschland steht zu seinen Werten	Germany stands by its values
andere Länder, andere Sitten	other countries, other customs
sie wohnen geballt in bestimmten Regionen	they live predominantly in certain areas
sie wissen nichts über die deutsche Lebensweise	they are ignorant of the German way of life
ihre Qualifikationen werden kaum anerkannt	their qualifications are rarely recognised
ganz andere kulturelle Gepflogenheiten	very different cultural practices
die gesellschaftliche Isolation	social isolation

8.3 Die Erfahrungen verschiedener Migrantengruppen

The experiences of various migrant groups

gut / schlecht abschneiden (irreg)	to come off well / badly
anmelden (tr)	to register
sich der Gesellschaft anpassen	to fit in with society
der Ansprechpartner (-)	contact person
die Arbeitskraft (¨e)	worker, employee
die Aufenthaltserlaubnis (-se) die Aufenthaltsgenehmigung (-en)	residence permit

ausbeuten	to exploit
ausnutzen	to take advantage of
behandeln	to treat, deal with
bestehen (*irreg*) auf (+*Dat*)	to insist on
die Bürokratie	bureaucracy
sich einleben	to settle down
erfinderisch	inventive
erledigen	to deal with
EU-Bürger (-)	EU citizen
fließend	fluent
gelingen* (i-a-u)	to succeed
es ist ihr gelungen, zu ...	she succeeded in…
gemischt	mixed
grauenhaft	terrible, appalling
der Grenzübergang (⁻e)	border crossing
groß werden* (i-u-o)	to grow up
sich hocharbeiten	to work one's way up
sich identifizieren mit (+*Dat*)	to identify with
die Identität	identity
der Lohn (⁻e)	wages
mieten / vermieten	to rent / to rent out
der Muslim (-e / -s)	Muslim (male)
die Muslime (-n) / die Muslimin (-nen)	Muslim (female)
der Nachzug	joining by family members (in Germany)
der Nahe Osten	the Middle East
aus dem Nahen Osten	from the Middle East
sich niederlassen (ä-ie-a)	to settle
die Not	need, poverty
Polen / polnisch	Poland / Polish
das Potenzial	potential
rechtfertigen	to justify
rücksichtslos	inconsiderate
der Schleuser (-)	people-smuggler
schwarzarbeiten	to work illegally, without a permit
die Sehnsucht (⁻e)	longing
sich sehnen nach (+*Dat*)	to long for
die Staatsangehörigkeit	citizenship
der Studiengang (⁻e)	university course
türkischstämmig	of Turkish origin / stock
die Überfahrt (-en)	crossing

überfallen (ä-ie-a) (*insep*)	to attack, mug
im Umgang mit (+*Dat*)	when dealing with
umstritten	controversial
die Unterlagen (*pl*)	documents, papers
der Unterstützungsbedarf	need for support
ursprünglich / der Ursprung (ᵈe)	originally / origin
versäumen	to miss, fail to have done, neglect
die Warteschlange (-n)	queue
sich wehren	to defend o.s.
sich weigern, etw. zu tun	to refuse to do sth.
das Zielland (ᵈer)	destination country
... steht Ihnen zu	you are entitled to…
zweisprachig	bilingual

in der Not schmeckt jedes Brot	beggars can't be choosers
Not macht erfinderisch	necessity is the mother of invention
jdm. Aufenthaltsverbot erteilen	to ban s.o. from staying in a country
aus Erfahrung lernen	to learn from experience
sein Asylantrag wurde anerkannt	his asylum application was accepted
eine andere Vorstellung davon haben (*irreg*), ...	to have a different idea…
... wie Staat, Religion und Gesellschaft zueinander stehen	…how state, religion and society relate to each other
an Recht und Gesetz halten (ä-ie-a)	to obey the rule of law
die doppelte Staatsbürgerschaft	dual nationality
die kulturelle Identität wahren	to keep one's cultural identity
Einwanderer (*pl*) der zweiten Generation	second-generation immigrants
Ehegatten folgen ihren Partnern	spouses join their partners

Websites

You will find other useful articles, links and vocabulary on this topic on the following websites:

www.bmi.bund.de/DE/themen/gesellschaft-integration/integration/integration-node.html (https://tinyurl.com/y96e9cju)
Federal 'Home Office'

www.deutschland.de/de/migration-und-integration

Strategy

Separable verb prefixes

The range of prefixes on nouns and verbs in German can appear confusing to begin with. Separable prefixes are always words in their own right, usually prepositions, sometimes adverbs. Always look at the root word first, then see what the prefix adds to the meaning.

A Was bedeuten die Grundwörter im Englischen? Was bedeuten sie mit dem jeweiligen vorangestellten Präfix?
1 wandern (ein-, aus-)
2 weisen (aus-, hin-, nach-)
3 bilden (aus-, fort-, um-)
4 schließen (ab-, an-, auf-, aus-)
5 steigen (aus-, berg-, um-)

Strategy

Noun genders

While it's important to learn the gender and plural of new nouns, there are patterns to both. For instance, male persons and professions, days of the week and most drinks are masculine, while most countries are neuter. Endings also sometimes provide a guide.
- **masculine endings:** *-ent, -ismus, -ist, -ling,* and most ending in *-er*
- **feminine endings:** *-ei, -ie, -heit, -keit, -schaft, -ion, -ung, -ik,* and many ending in *-e*
- **neuter endings:** *-chen, -ment, -um,* and many ending in *-nis, -ment, -tum*

B Wie würden Sie folgende Substantive einordnen: Maskulinum, Femininum oder Neutrum? Was bedeuten sie im Englischen? Es gibt einige Ausnahmen! Suchen Sie weitere Substantive mit diesen Endungen aus den Listen in diesem Kapitel.
1 Fähigkeit
2 Hindernis
3 Neuankömmling
4 Rassismus
5 Erlaubnis
6 Unternehmer
7 Integration
8 Opfer
9 Gesellschaft
10 Demokratie

9 Rassismus

angreifen (ei-i-i) / der Angriff (-e)	to attack /attack
die Angst (*pl* Ängste) vor (+*Dat*)	fear of
der Antisemitismus	antisemitism
die Ausländerfeindlichkeit ⎫ der Fremdenhass ⎭	hatred of foreigners, xenophobia
beleidigen / die Beleidigung (-en)	to insult / insult
von (+*Dat*) ... betroffen sein (*irreg*)	to be affected by...
die Einstellung (-en)	attitude
friedlich	peaceful
handeln	to act, take action
hassen / der Hass	to hate / hatred
herabwürdigen	to disparage, belittle
ignorieren / die Ignoranz	ignorant / ignorance
die Islamophobie	islamophobia
die Menschenrechte	human rights
die Minderheit (-en)	minority
misstrauen (+*Dat*) / das Misstrauen	to mistrust / mistrust
die Rassendiskriminierung	racial discrimination
Rassenvorurteile (*pl*) haben (*irreg*)	to be racially prejudiced
der Rassismus / rassistisch	racism / racist (*adj*)
rechtfertigen	to justify
schikanieren / die Schikane (-n)	to bully / harassment
terrorisieren	to terrorise
unerwünscht	unwanted, unwelcome
das Verbrechen (-)	crime
das Verhalten	behaviour
voreingenommen	prejudiced
das Vorurteil (-e)	prejudice

9.1 Die Opfer des Rassismus *The victims of racism*

Die Opfer — ***The victims***

der Asylant (-en)	asylum-seeker
das Asylantenheim (-e)	home for asylum-seekers
auffallen (ä-ie-a)	to stand out
auswandern*	to emigrate

demütigend	humiliating
ethnisch	ethnic
fürchten	to fear
die Hautfarbe (-n)	skin colour
die Herkunft (⁼e)	origin
hilflos / die Hilflosigkeit	helpless / helplessness
leiden (*irreg*) unter (+*Dat*)	to suffer from
die Ohnmacht	impotence, helplessness
das Opfer (-)	victim
die Sachbeschädigung	damage to property
der Schwarze (*adj. noun*)	black person
der Sündenbock	scapegoat
traumatisiert	traumatised
verletzt / die Verletzung (-en)	injured / injury
wegrennen* (e-a-a)	to run away
Die Täter	***The perpetrators***
die Affenlaute (*pl*)	monkey noises (racist chants at football matches)
der Alltagsrassismus	everyday racism
anfeinden	to treat with hostility
anpöbeln	to insult, harass
ausgrenzen / die Ausgrenzung	to exclude / exclusion
jdn. auslachen	to laugh at s.o.
die Ausschreitung (-en)	riot
bedrängen	to harass, attack
bedrohen / die Bedrohung (-en)	to threaten / threat
belästigen / die Belästigung (-en)	to harass, pester / harassment
beschimpfen	to insult
der Bombenanschlag (⁼e)	bomb attack
boshaft	malicious
der Brandanschlag (⁼e)	arson attack
einschüchtern / die Einschüchterung	to intimidate / intimidation
ermorden / der Mord (-e) an (+*Dat*)	to murder / murder (of)
die Gewalt	violence
die Gewaltdrohung (-en)	threat of violence
die Gewalttat (-en)	act of violence
gewalttätig	violent
Graffiti sprayen, sprühen	to spray graffiti
der Halbstarke (*adj. noun*)	teenage thug
die Kleinkriminalität	petty crime (activities)

konfrontieren	to confront
die Kriminalität	crime
der Kriminelle (*adj. noun*)	criminal
die Meinungsmache (*pej*)	propaganda
misshandeln	to mistreat
der Neonazi (-s)	neo-Nazi
provozieren	to provoke
die Rassenunruhen (*pl*)	racial disturbances
rassistisch motiviert	racially motivated
rechtsextrem / rechtsradikal	far-right
der Rechtsradikalismus	right-wing extremism
der Schlägertyp (-en)	thug
schubsen	to push, shove
stehlen (ie-a-o)	to steal
die Straftat (-en)	crime, criminal offence
eine Straftat begehen (*irreg*)	to commit a crime
der Täter (-)	perpetrator
treten (i-a-e)	to kick
verängstigen	to frighten, intimidate
vergraulen	to scare off
zusammenschlagen (ä-u-a)	to beat up

....

eine rassistische Äußerung fallen lassen (ä-ie-a)	to make a racist comment
Menschen (*pl*) afrikanischer / asiatischer Abstammung	people of African / Asian descent
sie werden wie Bürger (*pl*) zweiter Klasse behandelt	they are treated as second-class citizens
jdn. zum Sündenbock machen	to make s.o. the scapegoat
ein Verstoß gegen die Menschenrechte	an abuse of human rights
sie werden einfach nach ihrer Hautfarbe beurteilt	they're judged simply on the basis of the colour of their skin
jdn. in ein Klischee zwängen	to stereotype s.o.
jdn. als Sozialschmarotzer abstempeln	to pigeon-hole somebody as a scrounger
das gegenseitige Misstrauen	mutual distrust
der institutionelle Rassismus	institutional racism
etw. stillschweigend dulden	to tolerate, accept sth.
sie sind der Neonaziszene zuzurechnen	they're part of the neo-Nazi scene
fremdenfeindliche Parolen sprühen	to spray racist slogans

9.2 Die Ursprünge des Rassismus

The origins of racism

Rassismus in der Geschichte	Racism in history
die Bevölkerung (-en)	population
dunkelhäutig	dark-skinned
der Eingeborene (*adj. noun*)	native (of the country)
die Grundlage (-n)	basis
das Hakenkreuz (-e)	swastika
der Händler (-)	trader, dealer
die Herrenrasse (-n)	master-race
die Herrschaft (-en)	rule, reign
herrschend	dominant, prevailing
die Ideologie (-n)	ideology
der Jude (-n) / die Jüdin (-nen)	Jew
der Kolonialismus	colonialism
die Kolonialmacht (¨e)	colonial power
das Konzentrationslager (-)	concentration camp
ums Leben kommen* (o-a-o)	to die
die Niederlage (-n)	defeat
die Parole (-n)	slogan
die Rasse (-n)	race, people
die Rassentrennung	racial segregation
regimekritisch	critical (of regime)
das (Kaiser)reich (-e)	empire
der Rohstoff (-e)	mineral resource
der Siedler (-)	settler
die Sinti und Roma (*pl*)	Romanies (*pej.* Gypsies)
der Sklave (-n), die Sklavin (-nen)	slave
die Sklaverei	slavery
der Sturz (¨e)	fall / overthrow
stürzen (*tr*)	to overthrow
der Tod (-e)	death
zum Tode verurteilen	to condemn to death
töten	to kill
überlegen (*adj*) / die Überlegenheit	superior / superiority
unterdrücken (*insep*)	to suppress
der Untermensch (-en)	sub-human creature (Nazi term)
unterwerfen (i-a-o) (*insep*)	to conquer, subjugate
verfolgen	to persecute

verhaften	to arrest
vernichten	to destroy
versklaven	to enslave
vertreiben (ei-ie-ie)	to drive out
der Völkermord (-e)	genocide
der Wertstoff (-e)	resource
Widerstand leisten	to resist
die Zwangsarbeit	forced labour
zwingen (i-a-u)	to force

Rassistische Einstellungen	*Racist attitudes*
die Abneigung (-en)	aversion
der Andersartige (*adj. noun*)	someone who's different
Angst haben (*irreg*) vor (+*Dat*)	to be frightened of
anpassen	to fit in
aufrechterhalten (ä-ie-a)	to perpetuate
bestätigen	to validate, confirm
die Denkweise (-n)	mind-set
engstirnig	narrow-minded
erobern	to conquer
die Feindseligkeit	hostility
fremd	strange, unfamiliar
das Fremde	that which is strange
die Fremdheit	strangeness, unfamiliarity
gedankenlos	thoughtless
der Groll gegen (+*Acc*)	resentment, grudge against
herabsehen (ie-a-e) auf (+*Acc*)	to look down on
hetzen gegen (+*Acc*)	to stir up hatred against
minderwertig / die Minderwertigkeit	inferior / inferiority
jdn. misstrauisch betrachten	to view s.o. with suspicion
das Missverständnis (-se)	misunderstanding
missverstehen (*irreg*)	to misunderstand
der Neid	envy
stigmatisieren	to stigmatise
tief verwurzelt	deep-rooted
überfallen (ä-ie-a) (*insep*)	to attack
überleben (*insep*)	to survive
der Ursprung (¨e)	origin
die Verschwörung (-en)	conspiracy
die Verschwörungstheorie (-n)	conspiracy theory
verursachen / die Ursache (-n)	to cause / cause

widerwillig	reluctant, unwilling
wieder auftauchen	to resurface
das Wiederaufleben	resurgence
zerstören	to destroy

den Groll anfachen	to fuel resentment
Ängste ausnutzen	to play on fears
der kulturelle Konflikt	cultural conflict
auf Rassismus zurückzuführen	racially motivated
auf beiden Seiten	on both sides
Ausländer müssen als Sündenbock herhalten	foreigners are the scapegoat
ihnen werden negative Eigenschaften zugeschrieben	they're attributed with negative characteristics
ein ausländisch klingender Name	a foreign-sounding name
sie wissen nichts von anderen Kulturen	they're ignorant of other cultures

9.3 Der Kampf gegen Rassismus

The fight against racism

Offizielle Maßnahmen	*Official measures*
abhalten (ä-ie-a)	to deter
abschaffen / die Abschaffung	to abolish / abolition
der Anhänger (-)	supporter, fan
die Aufklärung	education, instruction
beseitigen / die Beseitigung (-en)	to abolish / abolition
ermitteln gegen (+Acc)	to investigate s.o.
die Ermittlung (-en)	investigation
erwischen	to catch, find out
festnehmen (*irreg*)	to arrest
das Gefängnis (-se)	prison
die Gerechtigkeit	justice
gleichberechtigt sein* (*irreg*)	to have equal rights
die Gleichberechtigung	equality
das Gremium (*pl* Gremien)	committee
das Hassverbrechen (-)	hate crime
die Menschenrechtslage	the human rights situation
die Nachrichtendienste	intelligence services
die Richtlinien	guidelines
der Terrorverdächtige (*adj. noun*)	terror suspect

für ungesetzlich erklären	to outlaw, make illegal
vorbeugen	to prevent
vorgehen* (*irreg*) gegen	to act, take action

Persönliche Maßnahmen — *Individual measures*

die Aufforderung (-en)	call (to do sth.)
die Beschwerde (-n)	complaint
besorgt / die Besorgnis (-se)	worried / concern
die Bewegung (-en)	movement (incl. political)
Brücken bauen	to build bridges
der Christ (-en) / christlich	Christian / Christian (*adj*)
demonstrieren / die Demonstration (-en)	to demonstrate / demonstration
Einstellungen ändern	to change attitudes
eintreten* (i-a-e) für (+*Acc*)	to stand up for
mit etw. fertig werden* (i-u-o)	to deal with sth.
das Flugblatt (⁻er)	leaflet
fordern	to demand
friedlich	peaceful
der Gemeindeleiter (-)	community leader
gewaltfrei	non-violent
das Gewissen	conscience
seinem Gewissen folgen*	to obey one's conscience
die Hilfsbereitschaft	helpfulness
isoliert / die Isolation	isolated / isolation
die Kampagne (-n)	campaign
kämpfen (*itr*)	to fight
bekämpfen (*tr*)	to fight (against sth.)
mutig / der Mut	courageous / courage
jdn. der Polizei melden	to report s.o. to the police
protestieren	to protest
reagieren	to react
selbstbewusst	self-confident, self-aware
die Solidarität	solidarity
Stereotypen hinterfragen (*insep*)	to challenge stereotypes
die Überzeugung (-en)	conviction, belief
die Verantwortung	responsibility
sich wehren gegen (+*Acc*)	to fight (against), resist
ein Zeichen setzen	to set an example
die Zivilcourage	courage (in standing up for one's beliefs)
die Zusammenarbeit	co-operation

die kulturelle Vielfalt	cultural diversity
ein verstärktes Bewusstsein für die kulturelle Vielfalt schaffen	to enhance awareness of cultural diversity
die Ausbreitung einer üblen Ideologie	the spread of an evil ideology
den Rassismus abbauen	to reduce racism
überholte Vorstellungen	out-dated ideas
auf Bundes- und Landesebene	at federal and land levels
das Ausmaß rassistischer Straftaten darf nicht verschleiert werden	the extent of racist crimes must not be covered up
man darf nicht schweigend zuschauen	you can't just look on in silence
wer nichts tut, macht mit	those who stand by and do nothing are complicit in the crime
die Würde des Menschen ist unantastbar	the dignity of each human is sacrosanct (§1 of German constitution)
das muss man sich (*Dat*) nicht gefallen lassen	you don't have to put up with it

Websites

You will find other useful articles, links and vocabulary on this topic on the following websites:

www.planet-wissen.de/geschichte/deutsche_geschichte/rassismus_deutschland/index.html (https://tinyurl.com/y7uflbwf)

www.verfassungsschutz.de/de/arbeitsfelder/af-rechtsextremismus/zahlen-und-fakten-rechtsextremismus (https://tinyurl.com/y8955yhm)

Strategy
Inseparable verb prefixes

Some verb prefixes are not words in their own right, so cannot be separated from the verb. The past participle of these verbs does not add **ge-**. The commonest inseparable prefixes are:

- **be-**: makes intransitive verbs transitive, or when forming verbs from nouns or adjectives
- **ent-**: suggests escaping, removing
- **er-**: suggests successful completion
- **miss-**: indicates 'wrongly'
- **ver-**: change of state; adding; finishing; 'away'; 'wrongly'; intensifies base verb

A Was bedeuten die Grundwörter? Was bedeuten sie mit Präfix? Finden Sie danach weitere Beispiele für Verben mit Präfix in den Listen in diesem Kapitel.
1 stehen – verstehen, bestehen auf, entstehen
2 ziehen – erziehen, verziehen
3 warten – erwarten
4 schreiben – beschreiben, verschreiben
5 brauchen – missbrauchen, verbrauchen
6 wickeln – entwickeln, verwickeln
7 raten – jdn. beraten, verraten

Strategy
Variable verb prefixes

A few prefixes can be separable or inseparable; the commonest are **durch-**, **über-**, **um-** and **unter-**. In pronunciation, separable verbs are stressed on the prefix (e.g. **wieder**sehen); inseparable verbs are stressed on the verb itself (e.g. wieder**holen**).

B Welche Verben verfügen über ein untrennbares Präfix? Was bedeuten sie im Englischen, und wie spricht man sie aus? Suchen Sie danach weitere untrennbare Verben aus den Listen in diesem Kapitel.
1 überfallen
2 umfallen
3 umbauen
4 unterstützen
5 unterdrücken
6 unterkommen
7 unterschreiben
8 überfallen
9 überleben
10 übersetzen

Theme 4   Aspects of political life in the German-speaking world

10 Deutschland und die Europäische Union

die Amtssprache (-n)	official language
das Anliegen (-)	matter of concern
der europäische Binnenmarkt	the European single market
Brüssel	Brussels
demokratisch / die Demokratie	democratic / democracy
einheitlich	uniform, the same
einig / vereint	united
die Einigung	unification
der Erfolg (-e)	success
die Errungenschaft (-en)	achievement
der Euro (-s)	the euro
Europa / der Europäer (-) / europäisch	Europe / European / European (*adj*)
die Freiheit (-en)	freedom
freiheitlich	liberal; based on principle of liberty
die Freizügigkeit	freedom of movement
der Frieden / friedlich	peace / peaceful
das Fundament (-e)	foundation
garantieren	to guarantee
gemeinsam	common, joint, mutual; together
die Grenze (-n)	border
der freie Handel	free trade
die Herausforderung (-en)	challenge
die Industrie (-n)	industry
der Krieg (-e)	war
die Macht (ˍe) / mächtig	power / powerful
das Mitglied (-er)	member
die Politik (-en)	politics (*sing*) / policy (*sing & pl*)
das Recht (-e) auf (+*Acc*)	the right to
der Staat (-en)	state
überqueren (*insep*)	to cross (e.g. border)
der Verbraucher (-)	consumer

die Währung (-en)	currency
die Wirtschaft (-en) / wirtschaftlich	economy / economic
der Wohlstand	prosperity, wealth
das Ziel (-e)	aim
die Zusammenarbeit	co-operation
der Zweck (-e)	purpose
die Europäische Union (EU)	the European Union (EU)
die Europäische Kommission	the European Commission
das Europäische Parlament	the European Parliament
die Europäische Zentralbank (EZB)	the European Central Bank (ECB)

10.1 Die Rolle Deutschlands in Europa   *Germany's role in Europe*

Politisches	*Political aspects*
das Abkommen (-)	agreement
anerkennen (e-a-a) / die Anerkennung	to recognise / recognition (official)
die Außenpolitik	foreign policy
austreten* (i-a-e) aus (+Dat)	to leave
der Austritt (-e)	leaving, exiting
beitreten* (i-a-e) (+Dat)	to join, enter into (agreement)
der Beitritt (-e)	entry, joining
die Bevölkerung (-en)	population
sich bewerben (i-a-o) um (+Acc)	to apply for
der Brexit	Brexit
das Bündnis (-se)	alliance
die Einheit	unity
sich einsetzen für (+Acc) / der Einsatz	to stand up for / commitment
die Feindseligkeit (-en)	animosity
der Frieden / friedlich	peace / peaceful
führen	to lead
die Führungsrolle (-n)	leadership role
Gehör finden (i-a-u)	to have a voice (politically)
gespalten	divided
gründen / die Gründung (-en)	to found / founding, foundation
das Gründungsmitglied (-er)	founder member
integrieren / die Integration	to integrate / integration
die Krise (-n)	crisis
die Sicherheit	security

sichern	to safeguard
sorgen für (+*Acc*)	to provide
der Vertrag (¨e)	treaty
auf der Weltbühne	on the world stage
das Volkentscheid (-e)	referendum

Wirtschaftliches	*Economic aspects*
sich ansiedeln	to establish (a business)
die Arbeitskräfte (*pl*)	workforce
die Dienstleistung (-en)	service
die Eurozone	the Euro zone
der Exportweltmeister (-)	leading exporter
der Konzern (-e)	group of companies
das Rettungspaket (-e)	bail-out package
die Sparmaßnahmen (*pl*)	savings ('austerity') measures
die Sparpolitik ⎱ die Austeritätspolitik ⎰	austerity policy
subventionieren / die Subvention (-en)	to subsidise / subsidy
das Unternehmen (-)	business, enterprise
das Wachstum	growth
die Waren	goods
die Wirtschaftsleistung	economic output
die Wirtschaftsmacht (¨e)	economic power
der Wirtschaftsraum (¨e)	economic area

Allgemeines	*Other aspects*
die Absicht (-en)	intention
aufgeben (i-a-e)	to give up
der Ausbau	extension, building up
beruhen auf (+*Dat*)	to be based on
ehemalig	former
entwickeln (*tr*) / sich entwickeln (*itr*)	to develop
die Erweiterung (-en)	expansion
die Folge (-n)	consequence
infolgedessen	as a consequence (of that)
in Kraft treten* (i-a-e)	to come into effect, force
die Nachkriegsjahre)	the post-war years
die Priorität (-en)	priority
die Rolle (-n)	role
schaffen (a-u-a)	to create
die Spannung (-en)	tension

stabil / die Stabilität	stable / stability
die Tagung (-en)	conference
die Verpflichtung (-en)	commitment
verstärken	to strengthen
die Vielfalt	variety
wachsen* (ä-u-a) (*itr*)	to grow
das Zentrum (*pl* Zentren)	centre
der Zusammenschluss (¨e)	joining together

dem Krieg ein Ende bereiten	to put an end to wars
gemeinsame Ziele verfolgen	to pursue common goals
in Vielfalt geeint	Unity in Diversity (EU motto)
in Frieden und Freiheit leben	to live at peace and in freedom
uns verbindet die Gemeinsamkeit unserer Interessen	we're united by our common interests
der freie Verkehr von Waren, Personen, Dienstleistungen und Kapital	the free movement of goods, labour, services and capital
Lösungen aufzwingen (i-a-u)	to impose solutions
das bevölkerungsreichste Land	the country with the largest population

10.2 Vor- und Nachteile der EU für Deutschland

Advantages and disadvantages of the EU for Germany

Vorteile	***Advantages***
abschaffen / die Abschaffung	to abolish / abolition
angehören	to belong to
der Austausch von Ideen	exchange of ideas
bereichern / die Bereicherung	to enrich / enrichment
beschäftigen / die Beschäftigung (-en)	to employ / employment
sich frei bewegen	to move freely
die Bildung	education
sich einigen auf (+*Acc*)	to agree on
die Energiesicherheit	energy security
ermöglichen	to make possible, enable
forschen / die Forschung	to research / research
die Währungsunion (-en)	currency union
der Zoll (¨e) / zollfrei	customs, duty / duty-free

Nachteile   *Disadvantages*
auslagern   to outsource, transfer abroad
das Hindernis (-se)   barrier, obstacle
die Identität   identity
der Kleinbetrieb (-e)   small business
der Kompromiss (-e)   compromise
der Landwirt (-e)   farmer
die Landwirtschaft   agriculture
die Souveränität   sovereignty
die Steuer (-n)   tax
Unmassen / Unmengen (*pl*) von (+*Dat*)   vast quantities of
die Verordnung (-en)   regulation
die Verschuldung   debt, indebtedness
verschwenden   to waste
die Verwaltung (-en)   administration
die Vorschrift (-en)   rule, regulation
   laut Vorschrift   according to the regulations
Zahlungen an die EU   payments to the EU

Allgemeines   *General*
alles in allem   on balance
anstellen / einstellen   to employ, take on
die Arbeitslosenquote (-n)   rate of unemployment
das Ausmaß (-e)   extent
das Auswärtige Amt   the Foreign Office
der Beamte (-n) (*adj. noun*),   official (= civil servant)
   die Beamtin (-nen)
der Bereich (-e)   area, sector
der Durchschnittsbürger (-)   average citizen
ersetzen   to replace
die Fachkraft (⁻e)   skilled worker
die Fortbildung   further training
die Gebühr (-en)   fee
gelten (i-a-o)   to be valid, in force
das Gesetz (-e)   law
die Gesetzgebung   legislation (making laws)
konkurrieren mit (+*Dat*)   to compete with
die Kultur (-en)   culture
die Massenproduktion   mass production
raten (ä-ie-a) (+*Dat*)   to advise
der Saisonarbeiter (-)   seasonal worker

übergreifend	general, overall
umfassend	comprehensive
unbestritten	undisputed
der Verbraucherschutz	consumer protection

Absatzmärkte sichern	to ensure markets (for one's goods)
ohne den Pass vorzeigen zu müssen	without having to show your passport
die Abschaffung von Grenzkontrollen	the abolition of border controls
Deutschland wird als Geldquelle angesehen	Germany is regarded as a source of money
Regeln und Bestimmungen	rules and regulations
die Spielregeln einhalten (ä-ie-a)	to play by the rules
sie nehmen es mit den Regeln nicht so genau	they bend the rules
ihre Interessen sind zu verschieden	their interests are too different
sich auf eine gemeinsame Politik einigen	to agree on a common policy
einen Kompromiss eingehen* (*irreg*)	to make a compromise
die Unterschiede sind gewaltig	the differences are huge
Was bringt sie uns?	What good does it do for us?
auf Konsens bauen	to build on consensus

10.3 Die Auswirkungen der EU-Erweiterung auf Deutschland

The effects of EU expansion on Germany

Wirtschaftliches	***Economic aspects***
der Arbeitnehmer (-)	employee
ausbeuten	to exploit
die Bestechlichkeit	corruption
die Bilanz (-en)	balance
Bilanz ziehen (*irreg*)	to take stock
die Finanzkrise (-n)	financial crisis
das Gehalt (¨er)	salary
der Gläubiger (-)	creditor
die Globalisierung	globalisation
der Handelspartner (-)	trading partner
die Konkurrenz	competition
die Korruption	corruption
die Lebensmittelerzeugung	food production

die Lebensqualität	quality of life
der Lebensstandard	living standards
der Lohn (¨e)	wage
nachhaltig	sustainable
der Ökonom (-en)	economist
Pleite gehen* (*irreg*)	to go bankrupt
schätzen (*itr*) / abschätzen (*tr*)	to estimate
das Wirtschaftswachstum	economic growth
der Wirtschaftswissenschaftler (-)	economist

Politisches, Soziales	***Political and social aspects***
abwägen	to weigh (A against B)
allmählich	gradual
der Antrag (¨e)	application
das Aufenthaltsrecht (-e)	right of residence
die Auswirkung (-en)	effect
die Bedingung (-en)	condition, requirement
begehrt	sought after
beharren auf (+*Dat*) / das Beharren	to insist on / insistence
beschränken / die Beschränkung (-en)	to limit, restrict / restriction
der Druck	pressure
einführen	to introduce
der Einwand (¨e)	objection
einen Einwand erheben (e-o-o)	to raise an objection
die Erweiterung (-en)	expansion
festlegen	to set, determine
flexibel / die Flexibilität	flexible / flexibility
der Flüchtling (-e)	refugee
gefährden / die Gefahr (-en)	to endanger / danger
die Gemeinschaft (-en)	community
grenzüberschreitend	cross-border
die Grundlage (-n)	basis
der Kern (-e)	heart, core
das Kriterium (*pl* Kriterien)	criterion (*pl* criteria)
der Menschenhandel	human trafficking
die Menschenrechte	human rights
die Minderheit (-en)	minority
missbrauchen	to abuse
die Missstände (*pl*)	abuses, bad state of affairs
mobil / die Mobilität	mobile / mobility
der Nachbar (-n)	neighbour

das Nachbarland (⸚er)	neighbouring country
das Stipendium (*pl* Stipendien)	grant (for students, researchers)
unterstützen (*insep*) / die Unterstützung	to support / support
sich verbinden (i-a-u)	to associate, unite
sich vergrößern	to get bigger
die Verhandlung (-en)	negotiation
vertiefen / die Vertiefung	to deepen / deepening
vertrauen (+*Dat*)	to trust
jdm. etw. verwehren	to refuse s.o. sth.
sich weigern	to refuse (to do sth.)
weltweit	global
der Widerspruch (⸚e)	objection / contradiction
die Zahl an (+*Dat*)	the number of
zugutekommen* (o-a-o) (+*Dat*)	to be of benefit to
sich zurückziehen (*irreg*)	to withdraw

der Begriff Europa	the concept of Europe
finanzielle Schwierigkeiten	financial problems
der Krieg gegen den Terror	the war against terror
bestimmte Voraussetzungen erfüllen	to meet certain conditions
niedrig bezahlte Jobs	low-paid jobs
eine engere Union	a closer union
das richtige Verhältnis zwischen A und B finden (i-a-u)	to find the right balance between A and B
die noch engere Zusammenarbeit	ever closer co-operation
die Investition in grüne Technologien	the investment in green technologies
nachhaltiges Wachstum	sustainable growth
die Kluft zwischen Arm und Reich	the gap between rich and poor
eine klare Absage an Extremismus, Hass und Gewalt	a clear rejection of extremism, hatred and violence

Websites

You will find other useful articles, links and vocabulary on this topic on the following websites:

www.europarl.de *European Parliament*

www.europa.eu *European Union*

www.bpb.de/politik/grundfragen/24-deutschland/40493/deutschland-in-der-eu (https://tinyurl.com/jbexxt6)

Strategy

Opposites

One way of expanding your vocabulary easily is to collect pairs of opposites. Make a note of them as they occur.

A Finden Sie Gegensätze zu folgenden Wörtern.
  1 zunehmen
  2 die Diktatur
  3 der Krieg
  4 austreten
  5 vereint, einig
  6 die Gefahr
  7 künftig
  8 zerstören
  9 schrumpfen
  10 einführen

Strategy

Nouns formed from verbs

Nouns formed from infinitives, or from an infinitive stem + **-ung**, are fairly obvious. There are, of course, many other nouns formed from or linked to verbs. Note them when you spot them.

B Mit welchen Verben sind die folgenden Substantive verbunden?
  1 der Zusammenschluss
  2 die Errungenschaft
  3 der Widerspruch
  4 der Begriff
  5 der Austritt
  6 der Einsatz
  7 die Verhandlung
  8 die Gültigkeit
  9 die Zunahme
  10 der Rückzug

11 Die Politik und die Jugend

der Abgeordnete (*adj. noun*)	MP (member of parliament)
die Ansicht (-en)	view (incl. political)
das Bedürfnis (-se)	need
sich befassen mit (+*Dat*)	to deal with, work on
jdn. befragen über (+*Acc*)	to ask s.o. about
der Bereich (-e)	area, field
die Demokratie (-n)	democracy
jdn. diskriminieren / die Diskriminierung	to discriminate against s.o. / discrimination
ehrlich / die Ehrlichkeit	honest / honesty
sich einsetzen für (+*Acc*)	to support
die Einstellung (-en)	attitude
die Gleichheit	equality
alle gleich behandeln	to treat everyone equally
die Grundlage (-n)	basis
die Jugend	young people
der Jugendliche (*adj. noun*)	young person
die Kampagne (-n)	campaign
kritisieren / die Kritik	to criticise / criticism
links / rechts (*adj*)	left-wing / right-wing
das Mitglied (-er) in (+*Dat*)	member of
die Parlamentswahl (-en) ⎫ die Bundestagswahl (-en) ⎭	general election
der Politiker (-)	politician
die Politikverdrossenheit	disenchantment with politics
die politische Partei (-en)	political party
die Regierung (-en)	government
die Steuer (-n)	tax
seine Stimme abgeben (i-a-e)	to (cast one's) vote
überzeugen / die Überzeugung (-en)	to convince / conviction
die Wahl (-en)	election
das Wahlalter erreichen	to reach voting age
der Wahlberechtigte (*adj. noun*)	person entitled to vote
Die Bundesrepublik Deutschland	***The Federal Republic of Germany***
der Bundeskanzler	Chancellor (= Prime Minister)
der Bundespräsident	Federal president
der Bundesrat	Upper House (cf. House of Lords)
die Bundesregierung	Federal Government

der Bundestag	Lower House (= House of Commons)
der Bundestagsabgeordnete (*adj. noun*)	member of parliament
das Grundgesetz	the German Constitution
der Landtag	federal state parliament
die Verfassung (-en)	constitution
das Verfassungsgericht	Constitutional Court

11.1 Politisches Engagement Jugendlicher

Political involvement by young people

Demokratische Organisationen	*Democratic organisations*
abstimmen / die Abstimmung (-en)	to vote / vote
der Ausschuss (¨e)	committee
der Beirat (¨e)	advisory council
beitreten* (i-a-e) (+*Dat*)	to join
bundesweit / auf Bundesebene	all over Germany / at national level
beteiligen an (+*Dat*)	to involve s.o. in
sich beteiligen an (+*Dat*)	to take part in
debattieren / die Debatte (-n)	to debate / debate
zur Debatte / Diskussion stehen (*irreg*)	to be open to debate
die Einsparung (-en)	cut-back, saving
eintreten* (i-a-e) in (+*Acc*)	to join
eine Entscheidung treffen (i-a-o)	to make a decision
der Freiwillige (*adj. noun*)	volunteer
der Freiwilligendienst	voluntary service
der Gegner (-)	opponent
gewinnen (i-a-o)	to win
die Kommunalwahl (-en)	local election
die Mehrheit (-en)	majority
die Minderheit (-en)	minority
der Rat (¨e)	council
der Sieg (-e)	victory
der Steuerzahler (-)	tax-payer
unterrepräsentiert	underrepresented
die Unterschriftenliste (-n)	petition
verbessern / die Verbesserung (-en)	to improve / improvement
verlieren (ie-o-o)	to lose
vor Ort	local

der Vorsitzende (*adj. noun*)	chairperson
das Wahlalter senken, herabsetzen	to lower the voting age
wahlberechtigt	entitled to vote
wählen (*itr/tr*)	to vote / to elect
der Wähler (-)	voter
das Wahlergebnis (-se)	election result
das Wählerverzeichnis (-se)	electoral register
die Wahlkabine (-n)	voting booth
das Wahllokal (-e)	polling station
das Wahlrecht	the right to vote
die Wahlurne (-n)	ballot box
der Wahlzettel (-)	ballot paper

Der politische Diskurs	*The political discourse*
der Aktivist (-en)	activist
die Angelegenheit (-en)	matter, issue
beeinflussen	to influence
der Befürworter (-)	advocate (of idea)
begeistern / die Begeisterung	to enthuse / enthusiasm
der Beitrag (-̈e)	contribution
einen Beitrag leisten	to make a contribution
beitragen (ä-u-a) zu (+*Dat*)	to contribute to
belanglos	trivial, irrelevant
sich beschäftigen mit (+*Dat*)	to be interested in, think about
sich beteiligen an (+*Dat*)	to participate in
sich bezeichnen als	to describe o.s. as…
diskutieren	to discuss
durchsetzen	to push through, enforce
einbeziehen (*irreg*)	to include, involve
der Einspruch (-̈e)	objection
Einspruch gegen (+*Acc*) erheben (e-o-o)	to object to
das Engagement	involvement, commitment
engagiert	involved, committed
gemeinsam haben (*irreg*)	to have in common
glaubwürdig	credible, believable
der Gleichgesinnte (*adj. noun*)	like-minded person
halten (ä-ie-a) von (+*Dat*)	to think of
herabsetzen	to lower / to disparage
der Heranwachsende (*adj. noun*)	adolescent
sich informieren über (*Acc*)	to find out about

minderjährig	minor, underage
nachvollziehen (*irreg*)	to comprehend, understand
die Null-Bock-Generation	disaffected youth
der Rat (*pl* Ratschläge)	(piece of) advice
rechtfertigen	to justify
eine Rede halten (ä-ie-a)	to give a speech
relevant	relevant
schaden (+*Dat*)	to damage
schimpfen über (+*Acc*)	to moan about
skeptisch / der Skeptiker (-)	sceptical / sceptic
tätig / die Tätigkeit (-en)	active / activity
das Thema (*pl* Themen)	subject, issue
etw. jdm. überlassen (ä-ie-a) (*insep*)	to leave it to s.o.
das Vertrauen / vertrauenswürdig	trust / trustworthy
vertreten (i-a-e) / der Vertreter (-)	to represent / representative
verworren (*adj*) / die Verworrenheit	confused / confusion
volljährig	of age
jdm. etw. vorwerfen (i-a-o)	to accuse s.o. of sth.
der Vorwurf (¨e)	accusation
werben (i-a-o) für (+*Acc*)	to campaign for, to advertise for
zuständig	responsible

sich politisch einmischen / engagieren	to get involved in politics
Unterschriften für / gegen (+*Acc*) sammeln	to organise a petition for / against
an Protestaktionen teilnehmen (*irreg*)	to take part in protests
ihre Interessen achten	to take note of their views
aus moralischen Gründen	for moral reasons
einer politischen Partei angehören	to be a member of a political party
sozial Schwächere (*adj. noun*)	disadvantaged members of society
ich habe mir vorgenommen, etw. zu tun	I've resolved to do sth.
mangelndes Engagement	a lack of commitment
um junge Wähler werben (i-a-o)	to try to attract young voters
auf nationaler / lokaler Ebene	at a national / local level
Deine Stimme zählt!	Your vote counts!
etw. aus Steuergeldern (*pl*) finanzieren	to pay for sth. from taxpayers' money
seine Vorstellungen in den politischen Diskurs einbringen (*irreg*)	to bring one's ideas to the political discourse
eine Demonstration veranstalten	to hold a demonstration

11.2 Schwerpunkte der Jugendpolitik

Emphases in youth politics

ablehnen	to reject
sich anmelden	to register
sich anpassen (+*Dat*)	to adapt to
auffordern	to challenge (s.o. to do sth.)
die Aufgabe (-n)	task
jdn. auf etw. (+*Acc*) aufmerksam machen	to make s.o. aware of sth.
der Beauftragte (*adj. noun*)	representative
beeinträchtigen	to impede, impair
der Begriff (-e)	concept
jdm. Beistand leisten	to give support to
benachteiligt	disadvantaged
berücksichtigen / die Berücksichtigung	to take into account / consideration
bestrafen	to punish
betreffen (i-a-o) (*tr*)	to affect, concern
betreuen / die Betreuung	to care, supervision
beurteilen	to judge, evaluate
ein brandaktuelles Problem	a burning issue
ehrenamtlich	voluntary
der Einheimische (*adj. noun*)	local person
sich einig sein* (*irreg*)	to be in agreement
wir sind uns darüber einig, dass ...	we are agreed that…
der Entscheidungsprozess (-e)	decision-making process
ernst nehmen (*irreg*)	to take seriously
das Flugblatt (⁻er)	leaflet
fordern / die Forderung (-en)	to demand, call for / demand
fördern / die Förderung	to support, encourage / support
gewährleisten	to guarantee, ensure
die Gewalt	violence
gezielt	specific, targeted
der Gleichaltrige (*adj. noun*)	peer
das Handlungsfeld (-er)	sphere of activity
Hürden abbauen	to reduce obstacles
investieren	to invest
ein Lippenbekenntnis ablegen	to pay lip-service
lobenswert	praiseworthy
Lösungen suchen	to look for solutions

Maßnahmen (pl) ergreifen (ei-i-i)	to take steps
der Missbrauch (¨e)	abuse, misuse
mitarbeiten bei (+Dat)	to work together on
mitbestimmen bei (+Dat)	to have an influence on
mitgestalten	to help to create
mitwirken an (+Dat) / die Mitwirkung	to be involved in / involvement
parteiunabhängig ⎤ parteilos ⎦	independent (of party)
in die Praxis umsetzen	to put into practice
der Querschnitt (-e)	cross-section
der Schwerpunkt (-e)	emphasis, main focus
Schwerpunkte setzen	to set priorities
die Sitzung (-en)	meeting
die Stadtverwaltung (-en)	town council
der Täter (-)	culprit
die Teilhabe	participation
die Veranstaltung (-en)	(organised) event
die Vernunft / vernünftig	common sense / sensible
die Verpflichtung (-en)	responsibility
verwirklichen	to fulfil, put into effect
verzichten auf (+Acc)	to go without
die Vorherrschaft	dominance
der Zugang (¨e)	access
das Zugeständnis (-se)	concession

....

eine zentrale Rolle spielen	to play a central role
ich bin mir bewusst, dass ...	I'm aware that…
das Freiwillige Soziale Jahr (FSJ)	year of voluntary community service
meine Arbeit ist was wert	my work is valuable
eine Diskussion auslösen	to provoke a discussion
Fragen von weitreichender Bedeutung	questions of far-reaching importance

11.3 Werte und Ideale   *Values and ideals*

Politische Themen   *Political matters*

abhängig / die Abhängigkeit	dependent / dependency
abschaffen / die Abschaffung	to abolish / abolition
arm / die Armut	poor / poverty
die Armutsfalle (-n)	poverty trap

die Armutsgrenze	poverty line
ausbilden / die Ausbildung	to train / training
die Ausgestoßenen (*adj. noun*)	society's rejects
ausgrenzen / die Ausgrenzung	to exclude / exclusion
der Behinderte (*adj. noun*)	disabled person
benachteiligt	disadvantaged
die Beschäftigungschancen	employment opportunities
die Bildungspolitik	education policy
das Bildungswesen	education system
die Chancengleichheit	equality of opportunity
die Einheit in Europa	European unity
das Entwicklungsland (⁻er)	developing country
erneuerbare Ressourcen	renewable resources
die Gerechtigkeit	justice
die psychische / geistige Gesundheit	mental health
das Gesundheitswesen	health care
die Gleichberechtigung	equality, equal rights
die Investition in (+Acc)	investment in
der Jugendschutz	protection of children and young people
der Klimawandel	climate change
die Konsumgesellschaft	the consumer society
der Leistungsdruck	pressure to achieve
die Menschenrechte	human rights
nachhaltig / die Nachhaltigkeit	sustainable / sustainability
die Obdachlosigkeit	homelessness
die politische Korrektheit	political correctness
der Populismus	populism
die Pressefreiheit	press freedom
die Ressourcen	resources
die soziale Gerechtigkeit	social justice
die Sozialleistungen	welfare benefits
die Sozialreform / die soziale Reform	social reform
die Besteuerung von Spitzenverdienern	the taxation of top earners
die Steuerhinterziehung	tax evasion
die Steuerumgehung	tax avoidance
der Terrorismus	terrorism
der Umweltschutz	environmental protection
die Umweltverschmutzung	environmental pollution
der Wohlstand	prosperity
der Zivildienst	community service

Allgemeines	*General matters*
die Aufmerksamkeit	attention
aufwachsen* (ä-u-a)	to grow up
die Auswirkung (-en) auf (+*Acc*)	effect on
etw. bekämpfen	to fight against sth.
die Belastung (-en)	stress, burden
der Bericht (-e)	report
bewirken	to bring about, achieve
jdm. etw. bewusst machen	to make s.o. aware of sth.
deutlich	clear, plain
der Einblick (-e) in (+*Acc*)	insight into
eingefleischt	confirmed, dyed-in-the-wool
erreichen	to achieve
erwecken (*tr*)	to awaken (e.g. interest)
friedlich	peaceful
glauben	to believe
sich einer Herausforderung stellen	to take up a challenge
hoffen / die Hoffnung (-en)	to hope / hope
idealistisch / der Idealismus	idealistic / idealism
die Integrität	integrity, honesty
das Interesse (-n)	interest
der Interessenverband (¨e)	interest group
kontrovers ⎱ umstritten ⎰	disputed, controversial
kurzfristig	short-term
langfristig	long-term
leiden (*irreg*) unter (+*Dat*)	to suffer from
die Leistung (-en)	achievement
naiv	naïve
in die Praxis umsetzen	to put into practice
das Prinzip (-ien)	principle
regeln	to regulate
retten	to save, rescue
die Selbstverwirklichung	self-fulfilment
sinnlos	senseless, pointless
sinnvoll	meaningful, sensible
sparsam	thrifty, economical
mit etw. (+*Dat*) sparsam umgehen* (*irreg*)	to use sth. economically
spenden / die Spende (-n)	to donate / donation

der Teufelskreis (-e)	vicious circle
den Teufelskreis durchbrechen (i-a-o)	to break the vicious circle
überproportional	disproportionate
unerträglich	unbearable
einen Unterschied machen	to make a difference
unterschiedlich	various, different
unterschreiben (ei-ie-ie) (insep) ⎫ unterzeichnen (insep) ⎭	to sign
verändern (tr) / sich verändern (itr)	to change, alter
vereinfachen	to simplify
vergünstigen (tr)	to improve, reduce in price
die Vergünstigung (-en)	privilege, benefit
vernachlässigen	to neglect
versprechen (i-a-o) / das Versprechen (-)	to promise / promise
den Vorrang vor (+Dat) haben (irreg)	to take priority (over)
vorziehen (irreg)	to prefer, give priority to
etwas Wertvolles	something useful, of value
wohlhabend	prosperous, well-off

der Kampf gegen Diskriminierung jeder Art	the fight against discrimination of any sort
die weniger Wohlhabenden (adj. noun)	the less well-off
die einkommensschwächsten Mitglieder der Gesellschaft	the least well-off members of society
die Rettung des Planeten	saving the planet
die IKT- / technologische Infrastruktur	(information and communications) technology infrastructure
die Gewinnbesteuerung in einer globalen Wirtschaft	taxation of profits in a global economy
allen Kindern, unabhängig von ihrer sozialen Herkunft, ihrem Geschlecht oder von Behinderungen, die gleichen Chancen bieten	to provide all children, regardless of their social background, gender or disabilities, with equal opportunities
unabhängig von Religion, Alter oder sexueller Ausrichtung	independent of religion, age or sexual orientation
einen existenzsichernden Lohn zahlen	to pay a living wage
auf dem Immobilienmarkt Fuß fassen	to get a foot on the property ladder
die Kluft zwischen Arm und Reich vermindern	to reduce the gap between rich and poor

den sozialen Zusammenhalt stärken	to build social cohesion
ein sinnvolles und durchsetzbares Abkommen erreichen	to reach a meaningful and enforceable agreement
ein Versprechen einhalten (ä-ie-a)	to keep a promise
Studiengebühren	university tuition fees**
das bringt mir persönlich was	it's valuable to me personally
eine dauerhafte Veränderung bewirken	to make a lasting change
etw. (*Dat*) ein Stück näherkommen* (o-a-o)	to move a step closer to sth.
sie sind besser informiert, was ... betrifft	they're better informed about…
es ist schon viel erreicht worden	much has already been achieved
es wird nicht genug gemacht	not enough is being done
es bleibt noch viel zu tun	there's still much to be done
außer Kontrolle geraten* (ä-ie-a)	to get out of control
die Debatte dreht sich darum, ob ...	the debate is about whether…
eine durchgreifende Reform fordern	to demand a complete reform
um ein Vielfaches geringer, höher	very much lower, higher
ihre Lebenschancen sind stark beeinträchtigt	their life-chances are much reduced
die künftige Politik muss darauf abzielen, ...	future policy must aim to…
er sieht den Wald vor lauter Bäumen nicht	he can't see the wood for the trees

** Note: German universities do not charge tuition fees.

Websites

You will find other useful articles, links and vocabulary on this topic on the following websites:

www.bpb.de/lernen/grafstat/142707/jugend-und-politik (https://tinyurl.com/ybfoo7f3)

www.focus.de/politik/praxistipps/wahl-o-mat-bundestagswahl-2017-wen-waehlen-sie_id_7449139.html (https://tinyurl.com/yah8xe6c)
Answer the questions and see which party suits you best – updated for every election.

Strategy

Adjectival nouns

Almost any adjective or participle can be used as a noun. Masculine and feminine forms refer to people, while the neuter forms (of which there are rather fewer) refer to abstract ideas. In use, adjectival nouns take the endings they would take if they were followed by *Mann* or *Frau* (or their plural).

A Stellen Sie fest, welches der folgenden Wörter **ein Adjektiv**, **ein Partizip 1** (Präsens), oder ein **Partizip 2** (Perfekt) ist. Dann bilden Sie ein Substantiv daraus.
1 jugendlich
2 deutsch
3 wahlberechtigt
4 vorsitzend
5 schwach
6 einheimisch
7 behindert
8 gleichaltrig
9 ausgestoßen
10 heranwachsend

Strategy

Verbs ending in *-ieren*

All languages borrow words from each other; German verbs ending in **-ieren** are usually French in origin, and while their endings have been thoroughly Germanised, there is no **ge-** in the past participle.

B Bilden Sie das Partizip 2 (Perfekt) und die Substantivform folgender Verben.
1 kritisieren
2 regieren
3 debattieren
4 engagieren
5 informieren
6 finanzieren
7 investieren
8 interessieren
9 organisieren
10 garantieren

12 Die Wiedervereinigung und ihre Folgen

autoritär	authoritarian
die Demokratie (-n) / demokratisch	democracy / democratic
die Demonstration (-en)	demonstration
fliehen* (ie-o-o) ⎫ fliehen* ⎬ flüchten* ⎭	to flee
die Folge (-n)	consequence
die Freiheit (-en)	freedom
die Grenze (-n)	border
der Kalte Krieg	the Cold War
der Kommunismus / kommunistisch	communism / communist (adj)
die Macht (¨e)	power
der Mauerfall	the fall of the Berlin Wall
die Meinungsfreiheit	freedom of expression, speech
die Regierung (-en)	government
der Sozialismus / sozialistisch	socialism / socialist (adj)
der Staatschef (-s)	head of state
trennen / die Trennung (-en)	to divide / division
überwachen (insep)	to keep under surveillance
die Währung (-en)	currency
die Wende	change (often = Reunification)
die Wiedervereinigung	reunification
die Wirtschaft (-en)	economy
Die Deutsche Demokratische Republik	***The German Democratic Republic***
die ehemalige DDR	what used to be the GDR
die neuen Bundesländer	the new federal states
die SED (Sozialistische Einheitspartei Deutschlands)	the SED (Socialist Unity Party of Germany) = Communist Party
die Stasi (Staatssicherheit)	Stasi (State Security) = secret police of the GDR
der Ostblock	the Eastern bloc (communist countries)

12.1 Friedliche Revolution in der DDR

Peaceful revolution in the GDR

Das Leben in der DDR	***Life in the GDR***
abhören	to bug (phone)
angreifen (ei-i-i)	to attack

einsperren	to imprison
der Fluchtversuch (-e)	attempt to escape
die Führung (-en)	leadership
der Grenzübergang (¨e)	border crossing-point
parteikonform	adhering to the (communist) party line
die Planwirtschaft	centrally planned economy
die Reisebeschränkung (-en)	travel restrictions
scheitern*	to fail
ein Schlupfloch dichtmachen	to close a loop-hole
die Sicherheitskräfte	security forces
der Spitzel (-)	spy
der Staatsfeind (-e)	enemy of the state
die Truppen	troops
der Überwachungsstaat (-en)	Big Brother state
unterdrücken (*insep*)	to oppress / to suppress
verhaften	to arrest

Die Revolution — *The revolution*

die Auseinanderzetzung (-en)	argument, dispute
der Ausreiseantrag (¨e)	application to leave the GDR
bedrohen / die Bedrohung (-en)	to threaten / threat
der Befehl (-e)	order, command
sich bemühen um (+*Acc*) / die Bemühung (-en)	to try to / effort
die Botschaft (en)	embassy
sich auf / über (+*Acc*) einigen	to reach agreement on
das Ereignis (-se)	event, occurrence
sich erinnern an (+*Acc*)	to remember, recall
jdn. erschießen (ie-o-o)	to shoot s.o.
die Feierlichkeiten	celebrations
feiern	to celebrate
der Flüchtlingsstrom	stream of refugees
fordern	to demand
die Freude	joy
die Friedensbewegung	the peace movement
das Friedensgebet (-e)	prayer-meeting for peace
friedlich	peaceful
die Gewalt / gewaltlos	violence / non-violent
gewalttätig	violent
das Gipfeltreffen (-)	summit meeting
hinter den Kulissen	behind the scenes

der Jahrestag (-e)	anniversary
der Jubel	jubilation
die Kundgebung (-en)	rally
ums Leben kommen* (o-a-o)	to die
machtlos	powerless
die Marktwirtschaft	market economy
etw. miterleben	to experience, live through sth.
öffnen / die Öffnung (-en)	to open / opening
die Pressekonferenz (-en)	press conference
der Protest (-e) / der Protestzug (-̈e)	protest / protest march
die Rede (-n)	speech
der Sonderzug (-̈e)	special train
teilnehmen (*irreg*) an (+*Dat*)	to take part in
der Teilnehmer (-)	participant
die Teilung (-en)	division
vereint	united
verkünden	to announce
der Vertreter (-)	representative
das Volk (-̈er)	the people / nation
vollziehen (*tr*) / sich vollziehen (*itr*) (*both irreg*)	to carry out / to happen
der Vorgang (-̈e)	course of events
das Vorgehen	action
die Wahl (-en)	election
einen Witz (-e) erzählen	to tell a joke
das Zeitalter (-)	era
der Zerfall	disintegration
zurücktreten* (i-a-e)	to step down
sich zurückziehen (*irreg*)	to withdraw
zusammenbrechen* (i-a-o)	to collapse

einen Ausreiseantrag stellen	to apply to leave the GDR
das geteilte / vereinte Deutschland	divided / united Germany
der Zwangsherrschaft entfliehen* (ie-o-o)	to flee tyranny
sie ließen sich nicht einschüchtern	they weren't intimidated
er wurde der Republikflucht für schuldig befunden	he was found guilty of leaving the GDR illegally
mit den Füßen abstimmen	to vote with one's feet (by leaving the GDR)

die Polizei ging gewaltsam gegen die Proteste vor — the police responded to the protests with violence

ich traute meinen Ohren / Augen nicht — I couldn't believe my ears / eyes

12.2 Die Wiedervereinigung – Wunsch und Wirklichkeit

Reunification – the desire and the reality

Negatives	*Negative aspects*
abschaffen	to abolish
arbeitslos / die Arbeitslosigkeit	unemployed / unemployment
die Arbeitslosenquote	unemployment rate
sich auflösen	to close down / disperse (*itr*)
etw. bemängeln	to find fault with…, criticise for…
das Defizit (-e) an (+*Dat*)	deficiency in
dichtmachen (*tr*) ⎫	to close down
stillgelegt werden* (i-u-o) ⎭	
dicht sein* (*irreg*)	to be closed
jdn. entlassen (ä-ie-a)	to fire, give s.o. the sack
der Geldmangel	lack of money
marode	ailing, ramshackle
veraltet	outdated, obsolete
der Verfall	ruin
verschweigen (ei-ie-ie)	to keep silent about
verwahrlost	neglected

Positives	*Positive aspects*
angleichen (ei-i-i) (*tr*)	to align
sich angleichen (ei-i-i)	to become more alike, grow closer
die Anschubfinanzierung	start-up funding
aufbauen / der Aufbau	to set up / construction, building up
beleben (*tr*)	to revive, reinvigorate
eigenständig	independent
einführen / die Einführung (-en)	to introduce / introduction
eingliedern	to integrate
in Erfüllung gehen* (*irreg*)	to be met, fulfilled
die Euphorie	euphoria
sich gewöhnen an (+*Acc*)	to get used to
modernisieren	to modernise
nachhaltig	sustainable

sanieren	to renovate
die Selbstbestimmung	self-determination
umdenken (*irreg*)	to change the way one thinks
die Vollbeschäftigung	full employment
das Wachstum	growth
Neutrales	*Neutral aspects*
befristen	to put a time limit on
der Bereich (-e)	field, area, sphere
bilden	to form
das Bruttoeinkommen	gross monthly income
das Eigentum (-e)	property
die Einkommenssteuer (-n)	income tax
die Einstellung (-en)	attitude
die Fabrik (-en)	factory
das Gehalt (¨er)	salary
grundverschieden	fundamentally different
die Lebenserwartung	life-expectancy
der Lohn (¨e)	wage
die Miete (-n)	rent
die Rente (-n)	pension
das Schlaraffenland	land of plenty
die Schwerindustrie (-n)	heavy industry
sorgen für (+*Acc*)	to look after
staatseigen (*adj*)	state-owned
die Steuer (-n)	tax
die Steuererhöhung (-en)	tax increase
der Steuerzahler (-)	taxpayer
die Stimmung (-en)	mood
umtauschen	to exchange (money)
umwandeln / die Umwandlung (-en)	to turn into / change, transformation
das Unternehmen (-)	company
unvorstellbar	unimaginable
verdienen / der Verdienst (-e)	to earn / earnings

die Kehrseite der Medaille	the other side of the coin
die Konjunktur ankurbeln	to boost the economy
„es war nicht alles schlecht"	"it wasn't all bad"
die öffentlichen Haushalte	the public finances
das hat niemand vorhergesehen	nobody foresaw that

es war für uns selbstverständlich, dass ...	we took it for granted that…
von der Wiege bis zur Bahre	from the cradle to the grave
besser verdienen (*irreg*)	to earn more
es hatte sich seit Jahrzenten nichts verändert	nothing had changed for decades
die Erstarrung der DDR-Wirtschaft	the GDR's economy's inability to change
eine Zeit der Unsicherheit	a time of uncertainty
sie wurden von der Arbeit freigestellt	they were laid off, made redundant
nur wenige trauerten der DDR nach	few mourned the end of the GDR
der Solidaritätszuschlag	extra income-tax on Germans to fund rebuilding of the former GDR
die soziale Marktwirtschaft	the social market economy (market economy with welfare state)
die Deutsche Mark (DM)	Deutschmark (currency which preceded the euro)
der Trabant / der Trabbi (-s)	East Germany's most common car
der Todesstreifen	the 'death strip' – mined no-man's land between E & W Germany and Berlin
die Ostalgie	nostalgia for aspects of life in the GDR
das Begrüßungsgeld	money given to East Germans coming to West Germany

12.3 Alte und neue Bundesländer – Kultur und Identität

The old and new federal states – culture and identity

das Agrarland	agricultural land
ähnlich / die Ähnlichkeit (-en)	similar / similarity
die Architektur	architecture
der Badeort (-e)	coastal resort
bedrückt	gloomy, despondent
begeistern / die Begeisterung	to inspire, enthuse / enthusiasm
die Besonderheit (-en)	peculiarity, special feature
bodenständig	long-established / down-to-earth
die Bundesregierung (-en)	Federal (state) government
dicht besiedelt	densely populated
dünn besiedelt	thinly populated
düster	drab, cheerless
ehemalig	former
erkennen (e-a-a) an (+*Dat*)	to recognise by

die Fahne (-n)	flag
feindlich	hostile
das Ferienziel (-e)	holiday destination
der Fortschritt (-e)	progress
die Gesinnung	way of thinking, outlook
der Hauptsitz (-e)	head office, HQ
die Hauptstadt (¨e)	capital city
die Hochtechnologie / Hitech-	high technology / hi-tech (*adj*)
die Kluft (¨e)	gulf, gap
die Küche	cuisine, style of cooking
die Kultur (-en)	culture
die Kulturlandschaft	cultural landscape
die Landesregierung (-en)	Land government
die Landsleute	compatriots
der Lebensstil	lifestyle
die Lebensweise	way of life
malerisch	picturesque
das Markenzeichen (-)	trade-mark
im Nachhinein	in retrospect
neidisch auf (+*Acc*)	envious / jealous of
pendeln	to commute
der Plattenbau (-ten)	prefabricated building (GDR)
die Polizei / der Polizist (-en)	the police / police officer
prägen	to characterise
regieren	to govern
reichhaltig	rich, varied
rückständig	backward
sich einer Sache (*Gen*) rühmen	to boast sth., pride o.s. on
der Rummel	hustle and bustle
spalten	to split
der Stacheldrahtzaun (¨e)	barbed-wire fence
das Stadtbild (-er)	cityscape
der Stadtstaat (-en)	federal state consisting of a city
der Statusverlust	loss of status
das Stereotyp (-en)	stereotype
der Tourismus	tourism
der Tourist (-en)	tourist
die Tradition (-en)	tradition
überwiegen (ie-o-o) (*insep*)	to outweigh / to predominate
überwinden (i-a-u) (*insep*)	to overcome

die Umwelt belasten	to pollute the environment
umziehen* (*irreg*) / der Umzug (ː e)	to move, relocate / relocation
unterschätzen (*insep*)	to underestimate
sich unterscheiden von (+*Dat*) ... durch (+*Acc*)	to differ from...by...
der Unterschied (-e)	difference
ursprünglich	original
vergleichen (ei-i-i) / der Vergleich (-e)	to compare / comparison
vermissen	to miss
verschwinden* (i-a-u)	to disappear
vertraut	familiar
eine Vielzahl an / von (+*Dat*)	a huge number of
etw. vorziehen (*irreg*)	to prefer sth.
der Wachturm (ː e)	watch-tower
das Wappen (-)	coat of arms
mit der Zeit gehen* (*irreg*)	to go with the times
der Zeuge (-n)	witness
die Zusammensetzung	composition
zusammenwachsen (ä-u-a)	to grow together

eine ländlich geprägte Region	a rural area
umweltbelastende Industrien	polluting industries
in seinen Traditionen stark verwurzelt	strongly rooted in its traditions
sie hält an ihren Traditionen fest	it holds on to its traditions
die Weichen (*pl*) stellen	to set the course

Websites

You will find other useful articles, links and vocabulary on this topic on the following websites:

www.zeitklicks.de/ddr/zeitklicks/zeit/politik/die-wende/
(https://tinyurl.com/ybv4b7md)

www.zdf.de/kinder/logo/die-wiedervereinigung-100.html
(https://tinyurl.com/ydcfn23v)

Strategy

Compound noun elements

There is an infinite number of possible compound nouns; new words for new concepts come into being all the time. Note down useful ones as you encounter them, remembering that the gender is always that of the last element (see Activities in Topics 3 and 6).

A Viele der unten genannten Substantive sind in den letzten Jahrzehnten entstanden, oder sie haben eine bestimmte Bedeutung während des Kalten Krieges erlangt. Notieren Sie, wie sie gebildet werden und was sie im Englischen bedeuten.

1 die Meinungsfreiheit
2 die Wiedervereinigung
3 der Überwachungsstaat
4 der Ausreiseantrag
5 die Umwelt

6 die Reisebeschränkung
7 die Zwangsherrschaft
8 die Vielzahl
9 der Stacheldrahtzaun
10 das Markenzeichen

Strategy

Working out noun gender from grammatical context

You want to use a noun from a text, but don't have a dictionary to hand to check the gender. Look carefully at the context of the noun to see what clues are given; remember that *der* is also used with feminine and plural nouns, and *des* and *dem* are used with both masculine and neuter nouns.

B Was können Sie dem Kontext über Geschlecht und Numerus der unterstrichenen Substantive entnehmen?

1 eine Zeit der Unsicherheit
2 sie haben einen besseren Verdienst
3 von der Wiege bis zur Bahre
4 sie entflohen der Zwangsherrschaft
5 viele haben mit den Füßen abgestimmt
6 die DDR war Teil des Ostblocks
7 das war ein erstaunliches Ereignis
8 leider ist er ums Leben gekommen
9 sie wurde der Republikflucht für schuldig befunden
10 mangelndes Engagement auf nationaler Ebene

C1 Sport

Sport

die körperliche Aktivität (-en)	physical activity
sich ausruhen	to relax, unwind
begeistert	enthusiastic, keen
sich Bewegung verschaffen	to get some exercise
der Druck	pressure
das Ergebnis (-se)	result
der Fan (-s)	fan
sich fit machen / halten (ä-ie-a)	to get fit / keep fit
gewinnen (i-a-o) / siegen	to win
die Mannschaft (-en)	team
die Meisterschaft (-en)	championship
der Profi (-s) / professionell (*adj*)	professional / professional (*adj*)
der Schläger (-)	bat, racquet, club etc.
das Spiel (-e)	match, game
spielen gegen (+*Acc*)	to play against
der Spieler (-)	player
der Sport (*pl* Sportarten)	sport
Sport treiben (ei-ie-ie)	to do sport
die Sporteinrichtungen	sports facilities
der Sportler (-)	sportsperson
das Sportzentrum (*pl* Sportzentren)	sports centre
das Stadion (*pl* Stadien)	stadium
teilnehmen (*irreg*) an (+*Dat*)	to take part in, participate in
der Tennisplatz (¨e), der Fußballplatz (¨e) usw.	tennis court, football pitch etc.
trainieren	to train
die Turnhalle (-n)	sports hall, gymnasium
verlieren (ie-o-o)	to lose

Sportler und Sportlerinnen

Sportsmen and -women

der Amateursportler (-) der Hobbysportler (-)	amateur sportsman
der Athlet (-en)	athlete
der behinderte Sportler (-)	sportsman with disabilities
der Fußballspieler (-) der Fußballer (-)	footballer, soccer player
der Profi-Fußballspieler (-)	professional footballer
der Gegner (-)	opponent
der Kapitän (-e)	captain
der Konkurrent (-en)	competitor, opponent
der Leistungssportler	performance athlete
der Linienrichter (-)	linesman
der Manager (-)	manager
das Mannschaftsmitglied (-er)	team member
der Schiedsrichter (-)	referee
Schiedsrichter sein* (*irreg*)	to referee
siegen / der Sieger (-)	to win / winner
der Spitzensportler (-)	top class sportsman
der Teilnehmer (-)	competitor, participant
der Torwart (-e)	goalkeeper
der Trainer (-)	trainer, coach
der Verlierer (-)	loser
der Weltumsegler (-)	round-the-world yachtsman

Sport und Wettbewerb

Sport and competition

ausscheiden* (ei-ie-ie)	to be knocked out (of competition)
der Ausscheidungskampf (-̈e)	knock-out competition
die Bundesliga	national (football) league
die erste Liga	premiership
das Elfmeterschießen (-)	penalty shoot-out (football)
das Endspiel um den Pokal das Pokalendspiel	cup final
entscheidend	winning (goal, point)
das Finale, Halbfinale (-)	final, semi-final
führen vorn liegen	to be in the lead
der Fußballrowdy (-s)	football hooligan
die Halbzeit	half-time
kämpfen gegen (+*Acc*)	to compete against
die Kommerzialisierung	commercialisation

der Kontaktsport (*pl* -sportarten)	contact sport
die Leichtathletik	(track and field) athletics
das Mannschaftsspiel (-e)	team sport
Mitglied in einem Verein sein* (*irreg*)	to belong to a club
die Nationalelf	national (football) team
die Nationalmannschaft (-en)	national team
die Niederlage (-n)	defeat
der Pokal (-e)	cup
randalieren	to go on the rampage
das Rennen (-)	race
der Rivale (-n)	rival
das Rowdytum	hooliganism
die Runde (-n)	round
der Sieg (-e)	victory
der Spielstand	score
der Sportplatz (⁻e)	sports ground
der Titel	title
das Turnier (-e)	tournament
der Vorlauf (⁻e)	heat
der Wettbewerb (-e) ⎤ der Wettkampf (⁻e) ⎦	competition
der Wettbewerbsgeist	competitive spirit
der Wettkampfsport (*pl* -sportarten) ⎤ der Leistungssport ⎦	competitive sport
der Wettlauf (⁻e)	race
das Wettschwimmen, Wettsegeln usw.	swimming, sailing competition etc.
das Ziel (-e)	finishing line
der Zuschauer (-)	spectator

ein Tor schießen (ie-o-o)	to score a goal
Spiel, Satz und Sieg an X	game, set and match to X
eine Niederlage erleiden (*irreg*)	to suffer a defeat
um die Meisterschaft kämpfen	to compete for the title
den Pokal gewinnen (i-a-o)	to win the cup
gegen jdn. laufen, schwimmen usw.	to race against someone
nicht in Form sein* (*irreg*)	to be off form, off one's game
ein Foul pfeifen (ei-i-i)	to whistle for a foul
den zweiten Platz belegen	to come second
an erster Stelle	in first place
auf Sieg spielen	to play for a win

das Ergebnis war 3 zu 0	the result was 3–0
mit 3 Toren vorn liegen	to be 3 goals up
das Spiel endete unentschieden	the match ended in a draw
unentschieden spielen	to draw
wir waren ihnen haushoch überlegen	we completely outperformed them
ich bin Mitglied in (+Dat)	I'm a member of
man braucht viel teure Ausrüstung	you need a lot of expensive kit
risikoreiche Sportarten	high-risk sports

Der Sportgeist — *Sportsmanship*

der Amateur (-e)	amateur
aufgeben (i-a-e)	to retire
betrügen (ü-o-o)	to cheat
disqualifizieren / ausschließen (ie-o-o)	to disqualify
das faire Verhalten / das Fair Play	fair play
die Herausforderung (-en)	challenge
manipulieren	to rig, fix
die Olympiade / die Olympischen Spiele	Olympic Games
der Olympiamedaillengewinner (-)	Olympic medallist
die Paralympischen Spiele	Paralympics
sponsern, der Sponsor (-en)	to sponsor, sponsor
das Sponsern	sponsorship
der Sportgeist / die Sportlichkeit	sportsmanship
der Teamgeist	team spirit
die Verletzung (-en)	injury
der Weltklassespieler (-)	world-class player
der Weltmeister (-)	world champion
der Weltrekordinhaber (-)	world record holder
das Wetten	betting

....

die internationale Verständigung fördern	to promote international understanding
den Rekord brechen (i-a-o)	to break the record
Sport ist ein Geschäft	sport is a business
die zunehmende Kommerzialisierung	growing commercialisation
sein Land vetreten (i-a-e)	to represent one's country
das Siegen wird zu wichtig	winning becomes too important

das intensive Training	intensive training
ein zweistündiges Training	a 2-hour training session
er geht jeden Tag zum Training	he goes for a work-out every day
ein Vermögen verdienen	to earn a fortune
er genießt Wettbewerbssituationen (*pl*)	he's a very competitive person

Drogen im Sport	*Drugs in sport*
sich aufputschen	to dope o.s.
das Aufputschmittel (-) das Stimulans (*pl* Stimulantia, Stimulanzien)	stimulant
die Dopingkontrolle (-n)	doping test
die Drogeneinnahme	drug-taking
der Drogenmissbrauch	drug abuse
die Langzeitwirkungen	the long-term effects
die Leistungsdroge (-n)	performance-enhancing drug
leistungsfördernd	performance-enhancing
muskelaufbauend	muscle-building
die Nebenwirkung (-en)	side-effect
die Probe (-n)	sample
das Risiko (*pl* Risiken)	risk
sauber	clean (of drugs)

verbotene Stoffe	banned substances
man fühlt sich unter einem enormen Druck	you feel under enormous pressure
die Drogen werden immer raffinierter	drugs are becoming more and more sophisticated
eine Urinprobe testen	to test a urine sample
eine vom IOC verbotene Substanz	substance banned by the IOC
bei einem Sportler eine Droge nachweisen (ei-ie-ie)	to prove that a sportsman has taken a drug
sie wurde positiv auf Drogen getestet	she tested positive for drugs
ihm droht eine bis zu zweijährige Wettkampfsperre	he's threatened with a two-year ban
seine Medaillen wurden aberkannt	he was stripped of his medals
in Tests nicht nachweisbar sein* (*irreg*) den Kontrollen entgehen* (*irreg*)	to be undetectable in tests
Athleten Kontrollen unterwerfen (I-a-o) (*Insep*)	to subject athletes to tests

Doping vertuschen	to conceal doping
die Gesundheit riskieren	to endanger one's health
Erfolg um jeden Preis	success at all costs

Vorteile des Sporttreibens	***Benefits of sport***
abnehmen (*irreg*)	to lose weight
Fett verbrennen (e-a-a)	to burn off fat
Fettpolster abbauen	to get rid of excess weight
im Freien	in the open air
die Freizeit	free time
die Freizeitaktivitäten	recreational activities
ein Wohlgefühl empfinden (i-a-u)	to have a feeling of well-being
die Lebensqualität verbessern	to improve one's quality of life
sportbegeistert / sportlich	keen on sport
sportlich aktiv sein* (*irreg*)	to do sport
Stress abbauen	to reduce stress
Zeit für sich haben (*irreg*)	to have time to o.s.

C2 Die Umwelt   *Environment*

das Abwasser	sewage
die Atomenergie ⎤ die Kernenergie ⎦	atomic energy
aussterben* (i-a-o)	to die out, become extinct
der Boden	soil
dreckig / schmutzig	dirty
die Energie / die Energiequelle (-n)	energy / energy source
Energie sparen	to save energy
die Erderwärmung	global warming
das Erdöl	oil
erneuerbar	renewable
die Folge (-n)	consequence
die Gefahr (-en)	danger
gefährlich / gefährden	dangerous / to endanger
die Gewässer (*pl*)	lakes and rivers
die Industrie (-n)	industry
die Katastrophe (-n)	catastrophe
der Klimawandel	climate change
die Konsumgesellschaft	consumer society
die Landwirtschaft	agriculture

die Luft	air
der Müll	rubbish, waste
nachhaltig / die Nachhaltigkeit	sustainable / sustainability
recyceln (*pf* hat ... recycelt)	to recycle
schaden (+*Dat*) / schädlich	to damage / damaging
schützen vor (+*Dat*)	to protect from
der See (-n)	lake
die See (-n) / das Meer (-e)	sea
die Umwelt	environment
die Umweltbelastung (-en)	damage to the environment
umweltfreundlich	environmentally friendly
der Umweltschutz	environmental protection
verbieten (ie-o-o)	to ban
der Verbraucher (-)	consumer
verschmutzen / belasten	to pollute
die Verschmutzung	pollution
wegwerfen (i-a-o)	to throw away

Die Probleme	*The problems*
die Ausbeutung	exploitation
freisetzen	to release
die Gefährdung (+*Gen*)	danger (to)
das Gift (-e), vergiften	poison, to poison
konsumieren, verbrauchen	to consume, use
künstlich	artificial
rücksichtslos	thoughtless
der Stromausfall	power failure, blackout
die Übervölkerung	overpopulation
umweltfeindlich	damaging to the environment
der Umweltsünder (-)	polluter
der Verbrennungsmotor (-en)	internal combustion engine
vergiften	to poison
vernichten / zerstören	to destroy
verpesten / verseuchen ⎫ verschmutzen / belasten ⎭	to pollute
verschwenden	to waste

es entsteht durch ...	it results from…
vom Menschen ausgelöst	man-made causes
wenn zu ihrer Rettung nichts unternommen wird	if nothing is done to save them

Die Folgen	The consequences
die Auswirkung (-en)	effect, consequence
bedrohen	to threaten
gesundheitsgefährdend	damaging to health
das Gewitter (-)	storm
katastrophal	catastrophic
der Treibhauseffekt	greenhouse effect
überleben (*insep*) / das Überleben	to survive / survival
die Überschwemmung (-en)	flood
unumkehrbar	irreversible
verursachen	to cause
die Verwüstung	devastation
warnen vor etw. (+*Dat*)	to warn of sth.
zurückgreifen (ei-i-i) auf (+*Acc*)	to fall back on

das Abschmelzen der Polkappen	melting of the ice-caps
der Anstieg des Meeresspiegels	rise in sea-level
die Überflutung der Küstenstreifen	flooding of coastal regions
vom Aussterben bedrohte Tierarten (*pl*)	species threatened with extinction
das ökologische Gleichgewicht gefährden	to threaten the ecological balance
beängstigende Ausmaße (*pl*) annehmen (*irreg*)	to reach a worrying level
bis zum Beginn des nächsten Jahrhunderts	by the beginning of the next century
die Bedrohung für die Menschheit	threat to humanity
in den Naturhaushalt eingreifen (ei-i-i)	to interfere with the balance of nature
man sagt voraus, dass ...	it is forecast that…
die Folgen voraussagen	to predict the consequences
die Folgen sind kaum absehbar	it's hard to say what the consequences will be
um kommender Generationen willen	for the sake of future generations
das wird uns teuer zu stehen kommen	that will cost us dear
es wird Millionen ins Elend stürzen	it will plunge millions into poverty
Was bleibt dann übrig?	What will be left?

Die Gegenmaßnahmen	Counter-measures
sich anstrengen	to increase one's efforts
den CO_2-Fußabdruck reduzieren	to reduce one's carbon footprint
der Elektroantrieb (-e) ⎫ der Elektromotor (-en) ⎭	electric motor
emissionsfrei	producing zero emissions (e.g. vehicle)
der Energiebedarf	energy requirements
die Energieeffizienz	energy efficiency
der Hybridantrieb (-e) ⎫ der Hybridmotor (-en) ⎭	hybrid motor
das Hybridauto (-s)	hybrid car
mindern	to reduce
null Emissionen	zero emissions
die Reichweite	range (e.g. of electric vehicle)
retten	to save, rescue
sparsam (im Verbrauch)	economical (in consumption)
mit etw. (+Dat) sparsam umgehen* (irreg)	to use sth. economically
die Steuervorteile	tax incentives
das Umweltbewusstsein	environmental awareness
das Umweltbundesamt	Department of the Environment (government)
die Umwelterziehung	environmental education
die Umweltpolitik	environmental policy
die Umweltsteuer (-n) ⎫ die Ökosteuer (-n) ⎭	environmental tax
der Umweltverstoß (⁼e)	action damaging to the environment
die Umweltzone (-n)	low-emission zone
die Verkehrsberuhigung	traffic-calming
sich zu etw. (+Dat) verpflichten	to commit o.s. to sth.
das Verständnis erhöhen	to increase one's understanding
vorsorglich	as a precaution

die Senkung der CO_2-Emissionen um 40 %	the reduction of CO_2 emissions by 40%
wir sind von (+Dat) ... abhängig	we depend on…
es gibt kein Zurück	there's no going back
Gegenmaßnahmen einleiten	to introduce counter-measures
grenzüberschreitende Regelungen	cross-border agreements

das Gesetz verschärfen	to tighten up the law
wir müssen schon entstandene Schäden (*pl*) beseitigen	we must repair damage which has already been done
die Schadstoffbelastung mindern	to reduce damage by pollutants
die Schäden (*pl*) eindämmen	to contain the damage
den Umweltschutz in die Praxis umsetzen	to put environmental conservation into practice
auf die Umweltverschmutzung aufmerksam machen	to raise awareness of environmental pollution
eine Wende in der öffentlichen Einstellung zum Umweltschutz	a change in the public's attitude to environmental conservation
ökonomische und ökologische Interessen abwägen	to balance economic and ecological interests
um das Überleben der Menschheit zu sichern	in order to ensure the survival of humanity
... stellt ein Problem für die Industrie dar	…represents a problem for industry
die langfristigen Auswirkungen bewerten	to assess the long-term effects
umweltfreundliche Produkte	environmentally friendly products
voll / frei von Schadstoffen	full / free of harmful substances

Die Luftverschmutzung — *Air pollution*

der Auspuff (-e)	exhaust pipe (of vehicle)
bleifrei tanken	to use unleaded petrol
die Brennstoffzelle (-n)	fuel cell
die Emission (-en)	emission (of gas etc.)
die Geschwindigkeitsbegrenzung (-en)	speed limit
das Gift (-e) / giftig	poison / poisonous
das Kohlendioxid	carbon dioxide, CO_2
der Kohlenstoff	carbon
der Krebsauslöser / krebserregend	cancer-causing agent / carcinogenic (*adj*)
das Ozonloch	hole in the ozone layer
quellen* (i-o-o) aus	to pour from
der Ruß / die Rußpartikel (-n)	soot / soot particle
der Sauerstoff	oxygen
das Schwefeldioxid	sulphur dioxide, SO_2
der Stickstoff / Stickstoffoxide	nitrogen / nitrogen oxides
der Wasserstoff	hydrogen

....

giftige Abgase abgeben	to give off poisonous waste gases
in die Atmosphäre blasen	to pump into the atmosphere

Autofahrer (*pl*) am Rasen hindern	to make drivers slow down
Autos müssen reduzierten Abgasnormen genügen	cars have to meet stricter exhaust controls
der geringe Benzinverbrauch	low fuel consumption
die Korrosionsschäden (*pl*) an Gebäuden	corrosion damage to buildings
ultraviolette (UV-)Strahlen	ultraviolet (UV) rays
ein vermehrtes Auftreten von Hautkrebs	an increased incidence of skin cancer

Fossile Brennstoffe	***Fossil fuels***
das Benzin	petrol, gas (USA)
der Brennstoff	fuel (e.g. for heating)
der Diesel(kraftstoff)	diesel (fuel)
der Energiebedarf	energy requirements
der Energieverbrauch	energy consumption
das Erdgas	natural gas
die Erdölförderländer	oil-producing countries
die Erdölförderung	oil production
die Erdölraffinerie (-n)	oil refinery
die Erdölvorräte	oil reserves
erschöpft werden* (i-u-o)	to run out
das Fracking, das Hydraulic Fracturing	fracking, hydraulic fracturing
die Kohle	coal
der Kraftstoff	fuel (for engine)
die Pipeline (-s) die Rohrleitung (-en)	pipeline
der Preis fiel auf x Dollar je Barrel	the price fell to $x a barrel
das Rohöl	crude oil
das Schiefergas	shale gas

Erneuerbare Energien	***Renewable energy sources***
Energie speichern	to store energy
alternative Energiequellen entwickeln	to develop alternative energy sources
energiesparend	energy-saving
die geothermische Energie	geothermal energy
die Gezeitenenergie	tidal power
nutzen	to use, make use of
regenerativ	renewable
die Solaranlage (-n)	solar energy system
die Sonnenenergie	solar energy

die Sonnenkollektoren	solar panels
der Stromer (-) (*inf*)	electric car
umweltverträglich	not harmful to the environment
verwirklichen	to put into effect, action
die Wasserkraft	hydroelectric power
die Wellenenergie	wave power
die Windenergie	wind power
die Windfarm (-en)	wind farm
die Windturbine (-n)	wind turbine

saubere Energietechnologien fördern	to support clean energy technologies
der Beitrag zum globalen Energieverbrauch	the contribution to global energy consumption
die grünen Zukunftstechnologien	the green technologies of the future
sie werden schon kommerziell betrieben	they are already in commercial use
sie können nicht kontinuierlich Energie liefern	they cannot supply energy continuously
ihr Einsatz wird durch (+*Acc*) ... eingeschränkt	their use is limited by...
der Ausbau dieser Anlagen ist vorgesehen	further building of these plants is planned
den Verbrauch auf das Nötigste beschränken	to limit consumption to the minimum

Energiesparen zu Hause	***Energy conservation at home***
dämmen	to insulate
die Doppelverglasung	double glazing
die Dreifachverglasung	triple glazing
große / geringe Energiegewinne	large / small energy savings
die Energiesparlampe (-n)	low energy light bulb
heizen	to heat
isolieren / die Isolierung	to insulate / insulation
lüften	to ventilate
das Passivhaus (ᐨer)	passive (= ultra-low energy) house
schonen	to conserve
auf etw. (+*Acc*) verzichten	to do without sth.
die Wärmedämmung	insulation (against heat loss)

die Regelanlage einstellen	to adjust the time / temperature unit
dadurch könnte man bis zu 20 % Energie sparen	by this method energy savings of up to 20% could be made
ein besserer Ausnutzungsgrad	more efficient use

C3 Erziehung und Ausbildung *Education and training*

das Abitur (*no pl*)	A-levels, Higher Grades
aufschreiben (ei-ie-ie) ⎫ notieren ⎭	to note down
sein Bestes tun (u-a-a)	to do one's best
ich bin gut in Englisch	I'm good at English
der Erfolg	success
erklären	to explain
die Erziehung	education, upbringing
die Ganztagsschule (-n)	all-day school
die Gesamtschule (-n)	comprehensive school
das Gymnasium (*pl* Gymnasien)	grammar school
der Lehrer (-)	teacher
der Lehrplan (¨e)	curriculum
man muss … / man darf nicht …	you must… / you must not…
gute Noten bekommen (o-a-o)	to get good marks
die Oberstufe	sixth form, years 12 and 13 (last 3 years of grammar school in Germany)
die Privatschule (-n)	private school
eine Prüfung (-en) ablegen / bestehen (*irreg*)	to sit / pass an exam
sich auf die Prüfungen vorbereiten	to prepare for the exams
zur Schule, Universität gehen* (*irreg*)	to go to school, university
die Schule verlassen (ä-ie-a)	to leave school
die Schulordnung	school rules
die Universität (-en) / die Uni (-s) (*inf*)	university
unterrichten / der Unterricht	to teach / lessons, teaching
wiederholen (*insep*)	to revise

Das Schulwesen	*The school system*
der Elternabend	parents' evening
die Fächerauswahl	choice of subjects
das gegliederte Schulsystem	secondary school system with different school types
die Grundschule (-n)	primary school
die Hauptschule (-n)	secondary school (10–15)
der Intensivkurs (-e)	intensive course
das Internat (-e)	boarding school
die Kernfächer	basic / core subjects

der Kindergarten (⸚)	kindergarten, nursery school
der Lehrermangel	shortage of teachers
das Leistungsfach (⸚er)	main A-level subject
Lesen, Schreiben und Rechnen	the 3 Rs
die Nachhilfestunde (-n)	extra tuition
die Orientierungsstufe	first 2 years of secondary education
das Pflichtfach (⸚er)	compulsory subject
die Realschule (-n)	secondary / technical school (10–16)
der Realschulabschluss ⎫ der Hauptschulabschluss ⎭	secondary school leaving certificate
die allgemeine Pflichtschulzeit	(period of) compulsory schooling
sitzen bleiben* (ei-ie-ie)	to repeat a year
die Stunde (-n)	lesson
das Wahlfach (⸚er)	optional subject

Lehrer und Schüler

Teachers and pupils

der Berufsberater (-)	careers adviser
der Fachleiter (-) für (+Acc)	head of department of
der Fremdsprachenassistent (-en)	language assistant
der Hausmeister (-)	caretaker
der Hausvater (⸚) / die Hausmutter (⸚)	housemaster / -mistress
der Internatsschüler (-)	boarding school pupil
das Kollegium	teaching staff
der (Studien)referendar (-e)	student teacher (grammar school)
der Schulabgänger (-)	school-leaver
der Schuldirektor (-en)	head (of secondary school)
der Schüler (-)	pupil, school student
der Schulleiter (-)	headmaster
der Student (-en)	university student

Die Prüfungen

Exams

der Abiturient (-en)	student taking A-levels
benoten	to mark, grade
er hat Mathe bestanden	he passed in maths
durchfallen* (ä-ie-a)	to fail an exam
er ist in Mathe durchgefallen	he failed in maths
er ist durchgerutscht	he scraped through
die Endnote	final mark
die Klassenarbeit (-en)	class test (continuous assessment)
eine Konkurrenzatmosphäre	a competitive atmosphere
die kontinuierliche Beurteilung	continuous assessment

der Leistungsdruck	pressure to achieve
leistungsorientiert	competitive (person, school)
mündlich, schriftlich	oral, written
der Notendurchschnitt	average mark (across subjects)
eine Prüfung wiederholen (*insep*)	to retake / resit an exam
einen Test schreiben (ei-ie-ie)	to sit a test
das Zeugnis (-se)	report

Der Lernprozess	*The learning process*
das Arbeitstier (-e)	workaholic
die Aufmerksamkeit	attentiveness
der Fehler (-)	mistake
das Gedächtnis	memory
ein fotografisches Gedächtnis	photographic memory
die Gedächtnishilfe (-n) /	memory aid / mnemonic
die Eselsbrücke (-n)	
der Hefter (-)	file
die Legasthenie /	dyslexia / dyslexic person
der Legastheniker (-)	
lernbehindert	with learning difficulties
die Lernstrategie (-n)	learning strategy
sich melden	to put up one's hand
Notizen machen	to make notes
pauken ⎤	
büffeln (*inf*) ⎦	to cram
stichwortartige Notizen	outline notes
der Streber (-)	swot
das Talent (-e), die Begabung (-en)	talent, gift
sich überarbeiten (*insep*)	to overwork

ich brauche immer Hintergrundmusik	I always need background music
ohne Fleiß kein Preis	no pain, no gain (*proverb*)

Der Unterricht	*Teaching*
abwechslungsreich	varied
das Arbeitsblatt (¨er)	worksheet
wir befassen uns mit ...	we're dealing with…
jdm. etw. beibringen (*irreg*)	to teach s.o. sth. (a skill)
bestrafen	to punish
Diskussionen (*pl*) fördern	to encourage discussion
die Disziplin aufrechterhalten (ä-ie-a)	to maintain discipline

die Disziplin straffen	to tighten up discipline
sich durchsetzen	to be assertive
gerecht, fair	fair
jeden gleichbehandeln	to treat everyone the same
konsequent	consistent
korrigieren	to mark
lasch / locker	lax / laid back
sich um ein Lehramt bewerben (i-a-o)	to apply for a teaching job
das Lehrbuch (ˉer)	textbook
ein gutes Lernklima	a good atmosphere for study
der Lernstoff	material to be learned
motivieren	to motivate
schwafeln (*inf*)	to waffle
unnahbar	distant, unapproachable
(Schüler (*pl*) / ein Fach) unterrichten	to teach (pupils / a subject)

....

die Kluft zwischen Theorie und Praxis	the gap between theory and practice
er kann sich nicht durchsetzen	he cannot control the class
er stellt hohe Ansprüche)	he sets high standards
er macht einen guten Unterricht	he teaches well
eine Beziehung zu seinen Schülern finden (i-a-u)	to relate to one's pupils
einen Schüler eine Stunde nachsitzen lassen (ä-ie-a)	to give a pupil an hour's detention
sie gibt uns Unterricht in Mathe	she teaches us maths

Das Hochschulsystem	***Higher education***
die Altphilologie	classics
die Anglistik	English studies
das Auswahlgespräch (-e)	selection interview
die Betriebswirtschaftslehre (BWL)	business studies
der Dozent (-en)	lecturer
dozieren über	to lecture on
sie hat Esprit	she's got wit
die Fachhochschule (-n)	tertiary technical college
die Fakultät (-en)	university faculty
Forschung betreiben (ei-ie-ie)	to do research
die Geisteswissenschaften	humanities
die Germanistik	German studies
der Hochschulabsolvent (-en)	graduate
die Hochschulbildung	higher education

der Hochschullehrer (-)	university lecturer
seinen Horizont erweitern	to broaden one's mind
der Hörsaal (*pl* Hörsäle)	lecture hall
Jura ⎫ die Rechtswissenschaft ⎭	law
einen Master machen	to do a Master's degree
die Naturwissenschaften	sciences
der Numerus clausus	restricted entry quota to university
promovieren	to do a doctorate, doctoral thesis
die Studentenbude (-n)	student digs, bedsit
das Studentenwohnheim (-e)	hall of residence, hostel
der Studienabschluss (¨e)	BA / BSc
das Studiendarlehen (-)	student loan
die Studiengebühren	tuition fees
der Studienplatz (¨e)	place at university
ich studiere Mathe	I'm doing a maths degree
studieren	to study, continue one's studies
das Studium	(programme of) studies
das Studium abbrechen (i-a-o)	to drop out of one's course
das Studium finanzieren	to finance a course of study
die Universität Bonn	University of Bonn
das Universitätsgelände (-)	campus
eine Vorlesung halten (ä-ie-a)	to give a lecture
die ZVS	≈ UCAS (clearing house for university places)

das Abitur berechtigt zum Studium an der Universität	A-levels give you the right to study at university
sich um einen Studienplatz bewerben (i-a-o)	to apply for a place at university
ein Fach intensiv studieren	to study a subject in depth
nach Abschluss des Studiums	after qualifying
einen akademischen Grad erhalten (ä-ie-a)	to get a degree
sie ist Dozentin für Geschichte	she lectures in history
dazu ist ein abgeschlossenes Hochschulstudium erforderlich	a degree is required for that
die gegenseitige Anerkennung von Hochschulabschlüssen	mutual recognition of university degrees (in EU countries)
man kriegt BAföG für Härtefälle (*pl*)	people get a grant in cases of hardship
die Uni frühzeitig verlassen (ä-ie-a)	to drop out of university

Die Sonderschule	*Special school*
die Blindenschrift	braille
die Chancengleichheit	equality of opportunity
lernbehindert	with learning difficulties
die Regelschule (-n)	mainstream school
die Zeichensprache	sign language

man nimmt auf ihre Behinderungen Rücksicht	they take account of their disabilities
man fördert die vorhandenen Fähigkeiten	they build on the abilities they have
Ausbildungschancen versäumen	to miss out on educational opportunities

Die Ausbildung	*Training*
die Abendschule	evening class, night school
das Abitur nachholen	to take A-levels later on
der Ausbildungsplatz (¨e)	position for trainee
das Ausbildungsprogramm (-e)	training scheme
der Auszubildende (*adj. noun*) ⎫ der Azubi (-s) (*inf*) ⎭	trainee, apprentice
berufsorientiert	work-orientated
die Berufsschule (-n)	training / F.E. college
die Einarbeitung	introductory training in company
die kaufmännische Ausbildung	business management training
die Lehre (-n) / der Lehrling (-e)	apprenticeship, training / apprentice
die Volkshochschule (-n)	adult education school
sich weiterbilden	to continue one's education / training
der zweite Bildungsweg	means of improving qualifications through night school etc.

man sollte mehr Ausbildungsplätze zur Verfügung stellen	more training places should be made available
der Mangel an Ausbildungsplätzen	lack of traineeships

Die Bildungspolitik	*Education policy*
am Arbeitsmarkt orientiert	orientated towards the job market
die Chancengleichheit	equality of opportunity
die Differenzierung	differentiation
der Etat für Schulen	state expenditure on schools
das hatte zur Folge, dass ...	the result of this has been that…
gut ausgestattet	well-equipped

die Klassenstärke senken	to reduce class sizes
das Lehrer-Schüler-Verhältnis	the teacher-pupil ratio
die Leistungen steigern	to raise standards
gravierende Leistungsmängel (*pl*)	serious underachievement
das nachlassende Leistungsniveau	falling standards (of achievement)
den Leistungsstand beurteilen	to assess achievement
die Lernmittelfreiheit	free choice of teaching materials
oben / unten auf der Prioritätenliste	high / low on the list of priorities
der Reformbedarf	the need for reform
grundlegende Reformen durchführen	to carry out fundamental reforms
sinkende Schülerzahlen	falling numbers of pupils
überfüllte Klassen	overcrowded classes

....

Bildung ist Ländersache	education is a matter for each Bundesland
den Leistungswettbewerb verstärken	to make things more competitive
Schüler zu geistiger Selbstständigkeit erziehen (*irreg*)	to educate pupils to think for themselves
die beherrschenden Themen der Bildungsdebatte	the main topics in the debate about education
die Erwartungen der Eltern erfüllen	to fulfil parental expectations
sie haben die Wahl zwischen mehreren Möglichkeiten	they have the choice of several possibilities
je nach Neigungen und Fähigkeiten	according to interests and abilities
es muss vorrangig behandelt werden	it must be given top priority
leistungsstarke Schüler sollten verstärkt gefördert werden	able pupils should be stretched
die soziale und berufliche Mobilität fördern	to encourage social and professional mobility

Section D
Welches Wort soll ich wählen?

Some English words have more than one possible German translation.

after
nach (+*Dat*) (*preposition*)	Nach der Pause ...
nachdem (*conjunction*)	Nachdem der Film zu Ende war, ...
nachher (*adverb*)	... und nachher ging er ins Café.

to appear, seem, look (see also 'look')
aussehen (= *have the appearance of*)	Er sieht krank aus.
scheinen (= *seem*)	Sie scheint ihn zu kennen.
erscheinen* (= *appear in view*)	Er ist in der Tür erschienen.
auftauchen* (= *appear after absence*)	Gestern tauchte er bei uns auf.

to ask
fragen (nach +*Dat*) (= *to ask about*)	Ich fragte ihn nach seiner Mutter.
eine Frage stellen (= *to ask a question*)	Er stellt eine Frage.
bitten (um +*Acc*) (= *to ask for sth.*)	Der Lehrer bittet um Ruhe.

before
vor (+*Dat*) (*preposition*)	vor dem Film ...
bevor (*conjunction*)	Bevor der Film angefangen hat, ...
zuvor (*adverb*)	ein paar Tage zuvor

to care, be careful
vorsichtig (= *cautious*)	Bei Schnee vorsichtig fahren!
sorgfältig (= *painstaking*)	Er lernt alles sorgfältig.
sorgen für (+*Acc*) (= *look after, provide for*)	Wir sorgen für unsere Kinder.
sich kümmern um (+*Acc*) (= *look after*)	Er kümmert sich um den Haushalt.
es ist mir egal (= *I don't care*)	Es ist mir egal, ob ...

to catch
fangen (= *to trap, catch, hold*)	einen Fisch / Ball fangen
erreichen (= *just catch e.g. a train*)	Erreichst du den Zug noch?

to change

ändern (*general*)	Ich habe meinen Plan geändert.
verändern (*appearance or nature*)	Sie wollte die Welt verändern.
wechseln (= *change money*)	Ich wechsele meine Euro in Pfund.
umschlagen (*weather, mood*)	Seine Stimmung schlug in Aggression um.
umsteigen (*trains*)	Auf der Fahrt nach Bonn muss man in Köln umsteigen.
(um)tauschen (*exchange, swap goods*)	Ich habe den Pullover gegen einen blauen umgetauscht.

to decide

beschließen (*general*)	Ich beschloss, ein Auto zu kaufen.
sich entscheiden (*between alternatives*)	Ich entschied mich für einen VW.
sich entschließen (= *to resolve*)	Ich entschloss mich, Musiker zu werden.

different

andere (= *different from the one mentioned before*)	Mein anderer Bruder ist etwas jünger.
unterschiedlich (= *varying*)	Die Wirkung ist unterschiedlich.
verschieden (= *different from one another*)	Mein Bruder und ich sind ganz verschieden.

to enjoy

(jdm.) gefallen (= *to be pleased with*)	Diese Musik gefällt mir sehr!
sich amüsieren (= *have a good time*)	Amüsiert euch gut!
Spaß an etw. (+*Dat*) haben (= *get pleasure from*)	Er hat Spaß an seinem Oldtimer.
Spaß machen (= *be fun*)	Der Abend hat uns Spaß gemacht.
genießen (= *to savour*)	einen guten Wein genießen

to feel

fühlen / empfinden (= *to feel / sense*)	Furcht / Hunger empfinden
sich fühlen (= *to feel + adverb*)	Ich fühle mich krank / unglücklich.

to get (Think of a synonym; a few of the many possibilities are as follows:)

werden* (= *become*)	Ich werde alt.
haben (= *own*)	Sie hat ihr erstes Auto.
bekommen (= *receive*)	Ich bekam heute einen Brief.

sich (+*Dat*) etw. anschaffen /
  besorgen (= *buy, obtain sth.*)
Ich muss mir einen Computer
  anschaffen / besorgen.
verdienen (= *earn*)
Sie verdient gutes Geld.

to know
kennen (= *be familiar with*)
jdn. / eine Stadt kennen
wissen (= *by learning / experience*)
Weißt du die Lösung?

to learn
lernen (*by study*)
Sie lernt Italienisch.
erfahren (= *find out*)
Ich erfuhr die Wahrheit.

to leave
(liegen) lassen (= *leave [behind]*)
Ich ließ alles zu Hause (liegen).
verlassen (*tr*) (= *leave, exit, quit*)
Ich verlasse das Haus um 8.
abfahren* (*itr*) (= *set off*)
Wir fahren um 8 ab.
überlassen (= *let s.o. see to*)
Überlass es mir!

to look (see also 'appear')
etw. ansehen (= *look at sth.*)
Sie sah sein Foto liebevoll an.
sich (*Dat*) etw. ansehen (= *have a
  look at sth.*)
Ich will mir diesen Film ansehen.
sehen auf (= *glance at*)
Ich sah auf meine Uhr.

number
die Nummer (*of house, phone*)
die Nummer meines Hauses
die Zahl (*mathematical*)
ein gutes Gedächtnis für Zahlen
die Anzahl (*indefinite*)
eine große Anzahl von Problemen
die Ziffer (= *numeral*)
arabische / römische Ziffern

only
erst (= *not before + time*)
Ich kann erst um 8 kommen.
nur (= *no more than + quantity*)
Ich habe nur wenig Zeit.
einzige (*adj*) (= *single*)
Er war der Einzige, der da war.

people
die Leute (*pl*) (= *group of people*)
Es sind sehr nette Leute.
die Menschen (*pl*) (= *people in
  general*)
Alle Menschen müssen sterben.
die Personen (*pl*) (= *individuals*)
eine Familie von sechs Personen
das Volk (= *nation*)
das deutsche Volk
viele (= *many people*)
Viele sind der Meinung, dass ...

to put
legen (= *lying down*)   Er legte das Buch auf den Tisch.
stellen (= *standing*)   Stell die Flasche auf den Tisch!
stecken (= *put into*)   Er steckt die Hand in die Tasche.
tun (*in general* – *inf*)   Tu die Tassen in den Schrank!

same
gleich (= *alike, equal*)   Wir tragen die gleiche Hose.
(der)selbe (= *self / same*)   Wir haben dieselbe Mutter.

to stay
bleiben* (= *remain in one place / condition*)   Er blieb den ganzen Tag bei uns.
wohnen / sich aufhalten (= *be based temporarily*)   Er hält sich im Hotel auf.
verbringen (= *spend time*)   Ich verbringe 3 Tage in den USA.
übernachten (= *stay the night*)   Du kannst bei uns übernachten.

to stop
halten (*itr*) (= *halt*)   Der Bus hält hier.
anhalten (*tr / itr*) (*temporary, unexpected*)   Plötzlich hielt er das Auto an.
aufhalten (*tr*) (= *delay, hinder*)   Der Streik hält den Brief auf.
aufhören (*itr*) (= *stop doing sth.*)   Es hörte auf zu regnen.

to take
nehmen (= *pick up, use*)   Nimm den Zug / dieses Buch!
bringen (*someone somewhere*)   Ich bringe dich zum Bahnhof.
dauern (*time*)   Die Reise hat 2 Stunden gedauert.

there is / are (much less used in German than English; avoid where possible)
es gibt (*general*)   Es gibt einen Gott. (Gott existiert.)
es ist / sind (*specific time, place*)   Es ist ein Mann im Auto. (Ein Mann sitzt ...)

thing
die Sache (-n) (= *possession*)   Hast du deine Sachen mit?
(= *affair, subject*)   Sport ist nicht meine Sache.
das Ding (*object*)   Was ist das für ein Ding?
(*pl* = *serious matters*)   Diese Dinge gehen nur mich an.

the + adjective + thing	Das Beste / Schlimmste ist, ...
not a thing	überhaupt nichts
to do one's own thing	seinen eigenen Weg gehen

to think

denken an (= have in mind)	Woran denkst du?
denken / halten von (= have an opinion on)	Was hältst du von ihm?
halten für (= consider to be)	Ich halte es für das Beste, wenn ...
nachdenken über (= weigh up)	Ich muss darüber nachdenken, ob ...
meinen (= give an opinion)	Ich meine, es wäre besser, wenn ...

time

die Zeit (-en) (period)	Ich habe keine Zeit dazu.
das Mal (-e) (occasion)	Sie ist zum ersten Mal hier.
jdm. Spaß machen (a good time)	Es hat mir Spaß gemacht!

to (+ place)

nach (+ town, country)	Wir fahren nach Kiel / nach Irland.
zu (to a destination)	Ich fahre zur Schule.
in (implies 'into')	Ich gehe in die Stadt / ins Kino / ins Konzert / in die Schule.

to try

versuchen (= attempt)	Ich versuchte, ihm zu helfen.
probieren (= sample)	Probieren Sie diesen Wein!
an-/ausprobieren (= try on / out)	Hast du diese Methode ausprobiert?

to use

benutzen, verwenden (= to utilise)	Ich benutze immer ein Wörterbuch.
gebrauchen (= utilise sth. one has)	Er gebraucht einen Kuli.
nutzen (= to exploit, positively)	Sie nutzt jede Chance.
ausnutzen (= to exploit, negatively)	Er nutzt ihre Gutmütigkeit aus.
anwenden (= to apply)	Sie hat diese Methode angewandt.
verbrauchen (= to consume)	Dieses Auto verbraucht viel Benzin.

to work

arbeiten (= labour)	Sie hat sich nach oben gearbeitet.
funktionieren, gehen (= function)	Meine Uhr geht nicht.
klappen (= to work out) (inf)	Ich hoffe, dass es klappt.
ausdenken (to work out scheme)	Ich muss mir einen Plan ausdenken.

Section E

Zeitausdrücke

E1 Die Vergangenheit

The past

2006 / im Jahr 2006	in 2006
anno dazumal	in the old days
bis jetzt	until now
bis vor kurzem	until recently
damals	in those days, then
das ist schon seit jeher so	it's always been like that
erst gestern	not until / only yesterday
in den 70er Jahren	in the 1970s
in den letzten paar Jahren	in the last few years
in der guten alten Zeit	in the good old days
in letzter Zeit	recently (up to now)
längst	for a long time (past)
neulich	recently (not very long ago)
seit ewigen Zeiten	for ages
von Anfang an	right from the start
vor mehreren Jahren	several years ago
zu der Zeit, als ...	at a time when…

E2 Die Gegenwart

The present

aktuell	up-to-date, current
es ist höchste Zeit, dass ...	it's high time that…
gleichzeitig	at the same time
heutzutage	nowadays
im 21. Jahrhundert	in the 21st century
im Anfangsstadium	in the early stages
in der Nacht zum 24. Juli	on the night of 23 July
inzwischen	in the meantime
mit der Zeit gehen* (irreg)	to move with the times
momentan	at present
vorläufig	for the time being

E3 Die Zukunft — *The future*

auf unbestimmte Zeit	for an indefinite period of time
früher oder später	sooner or later
für alle Zeiten	for all time
im Voraus	in advance
in naher Zukunft	in the near future
mit der Zeit	in (the course of) time
möglichst bald	as soon as possible
über Nacht	overnight
Versäumtes nachholen	to make up for lost time
von jetzt an / in Zukunft	from now on / in future
vorzeitig	ahead of time

E4 Verschiedenes — *Miscellaneous phrases*

alle 10 Minuten	every 10 minutes
das ganze Jahr über	all year round
den ganzen Tag	all day
er ist in den Vierzigern	he's in his forties
fast die ganze Zeit	most of the time
gelegentlich	occasionally
immer wieder	again and again
in den mittleren Jahren, mittleren Alters	middle-aged
jede halbe Stunde	every half an hour
jeden zweiten Tag	every other day
mit den Jahren	as one gets older, as time goes by
nach und nach	bit by bit, gradually
sie ist Anfang / Mitte / Ende zwanzig	she's in her early / mid / late twenties
tagaus, tagein	day in, day out
zu jeder Zeit	at any time
zum ersten Mal	for the first time